DK EYE

WESTCHESTER PUBL

601 9100 660 069 0

P9-EMH-508

TOP 10
WASHINGTON, DC

Top 10 Washington, DC Highlights

Welcome to Washington, DC.........**5**

Exploring Washington, DC............**6**

Washington, DC's Highlights.......**10**

United States Capitol...................**12**

The White House.........................**16**

National Air and
Space Museum.........................**20**

National Museum
of American History.................**22**

National Gallery of Art...............**24**

National Museum
of Natural History....................**28**

Washington National
Cathedral...............................**30**

National Museum
of African American
History and Culture.................**32**

Arlington National Cemetery......**34**

Mount Vernon.............................**36**

The Top 10 of Everything

Moments in History.....................**42**

US Presidents.............................**44**

Places of African
American History....................**46**

Historic Homes and Buildings....**48**

Memorials and Monuments.......**50**

Museums....................................**54**

Art Galleries...............................**56**

Green Spaces.............................**58**

Outdoor Activities......................**60**

Off the Beaten Path....................**62**

Children's Attractions.................**64**

Theaters.....................................**66**

Restaurants................................**68**

Washington, DC for Free............**70**

Festivals and Cultural Events.....**72**

Trips from Washington, DC.........**74**

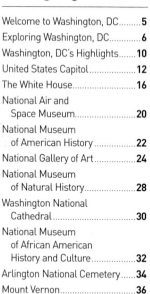

CONTENTS

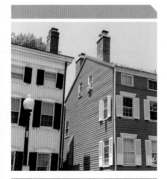

Washington, DC Area by Area

Around Capitol Hill.......................**78**

The National Mall.........................**84**

Penn Quarter................................**94**

The White House
and Foggy Bottom.....................**98**

Georgetown................................**104**

Beyond the City Center..............**110**

Streetsmart

Getting Around............................**118**

Practical Information...................**122**

Places to Stay..............................**126**

General Index..............................**134**

Acknowledgments.......................**142**

Street Index................................**144**

Within each Top 10 list in this book, no hierarchy of quality or popularity is implied. All 10 are, in the editor's opinion, of roughly equal merit.
   Throughout this book, floors are referred to in accordance with American usage; i.e., the "first floor" is at ground level.

Title page, front cover and spine
Cherry Blossom Festival at the Jefferson Memorial
Back cover, clockwise from top left
Georgetown; Key Bridge, Potomac River; the Washington Monument; Jefferson Memorial; statue of Abraham Lincoln, US Capitol

The rapid rate at which the world is changing is constantly keeping the DK Eyewitness team on our toes. While we've worked hard to ensure that this edition of Washington, DC is accurate and up-to-date, we know that opening hours alter, standards shift, prices fluctuate, places close and new ones pop up in their stead. So, if you notice we've got something wrong or left something out, we want to hear about it. Please get in touch at **travelguides@dk.com**

FREEDOM OF SPEECH
FREEDOM OF WORSHIP
FREEDOM FROM WANT
FREEDOM FROM FEAR

Welcome to
Washington, DC

City of politics and power. City of intrigue, passion, and history. World-renowned museums and monuments, broad avenues, vast green spaces, and breathtaking architecture combine to make this one of the most beautiful, captivating, and exciting cities in the world. With DK Eyewitness Top 10 Washington, DC, it's yours to explore.

What's not to love in a city where so much, including 19 Smithsonian museums and galleries, along with scores of monuments, memorials, and even government buildings, is open to the public free of charge? Everyone starts at the **National Mall**, the museum-and-monument-filled park that's the heart of the capital. You'll be able to discover dinosaurs and diamonds at the **National Museum of Natural History**; peruse Monets and Rembrandts in the **National Gallery of Art**; be inspired by great words at the **Lincoln Memorial**; and see the city at your feet from the top of the **Washington Monument**.

Beyond the Mall, a cornucopia of shopping, dining, and adventure awaits you – from the elegant boutiques of **Georgetown**, to the cafés of **U Street** and **Adams Morgan**, to the green spaces and blossom-lined trails of the National Arboretum and East Potomac Park. And, of course, when you are ready to eat, you'll find the city overflowing with excellent restaurants serving international and local cuisines for every budget and palate.

Whether you're visiting for a weekend or a week, our Top 10 guide brings together the best of everything that Washington, DC has to offer. The guide gives you useful tips throughout, from seeking out what's free to discovering places off the beaten path, plus seven easy-to-follow itineraries designed to tie together a clutch of sights in a short space of time. Add inspiring photography and detailed maps, and you've got the essential pocket-sized travel companion. **Enjoy the book, and enjoy Washington, DC**.

Clockwise from top: **Jefferson Memorial, Washington Monument, the North Apse in the Basilica of the National Shrine of the Immaculate Conception, the South Lawn of the White House, Martin Luther King, Jr. Memorial, quote from Franklin Delano Roosevelt Memorial, Georgetown row houses, Lincoln Memorial**

Exploring Washington, DC

Whether you have just a couple of days, or more time to explore, there's so much to see and do in America's capital city that you will want to make every minute count. The city is easy to get around on foot, with the Metrorail a fast and efficient alternative. These two- and four-day itineraries will help you make the most of your time.

from National Zoo and Washington National Cathedral 2 miles (3 km)

Dumbarton Oaks

Wisconsin Street

1789

Georgetown

M Street

Kennedy Center

The White House is the residence of the president, as well as the seat of executive power.

Key
— Two-day itinerary
— Four-day itinerary

2amys
Washington National Cathedral — National Zoo
Arlington National Cemetery
Area of main map
METRO
Old Town Alexandria
George Washington's Distillery
Mount Vernon

Two Days in Washington, DC

Day ❶
MORNING
Spend the morning at the **National Air and Space Museum** (see pp20–21) making sure to see the 1903 *Wright Flyer* and Neil Armstrong's Apollo 11 spacesuit. Lunch at **Pavilion Café** (see p91).

AFTERNOON
Walk to the **White House** (see pp16–19) then stroll south and take the elevator up to the **Washington Monument** (see p87) to enjoy the views. Next, head west to the **Lincoln Memorial** (see p86) and the **Jefferson Memorial** (see p88). In the evening see a show at the **Kennedy Center** (see p99).

Day ❷
MORNING
Start at the **National Museum of Natural History** (see pp28–9) then go next door to the **National Museum of American History** (see pp22–3).

AFTERNOON
Head to the **US Capitol** (see pp12–15) and take the Capitol tour, followed by an amble through the lush **US Botanic Garden Conservatory** (see p80). Have dinner (see p97) in Penn Quarter, then stroll in the Mall to see the monuments lit up at night.

Four Days in Washington, DC

Day ❶
MORNING
Visit the **National Museum of American History** (see pp22–3). Then stroll east on the Mall to the **National Gallery of Art** (see pp24–7) and have lunch in the **Cascade Café** (see p91).

AFTERNOON
Take the guided tour of the **Library of Congress** (see p79). Then head to the Visitor Center of the **US Capitol** (see pp12–15), and get a ticket for the tour.

The National Museum of Natural History captivates visitors, especially children, with its lively exhibits.

The White House

Vietnam Veteran's Memorial

Lincoln Memorial

Nat. Museum of Natural History

National Sculpture Garden

Penn Quarter

Nat. Gallery of Art

US Capitol Visitors Center

Library of Congress

Washington Monument

Nat. Museum of American History

Nat. Air and Space Museum

Mitsitam Café

US Botanic Garden Conservatory

Jefferson Memorial

CA6

potomac

0 kilometers   1

0 miles   0.5

The Library of Congress is the largest in the world, housing over 120 million items in a grand setting.

Day ❷

MORNING

Visit the **National Air and Space Museum** (*see pp20–21*) early, then cross the Mall to the **National Museum of Natural History** (*see pp28–9*). Have lunch at **Mitsitam Café** (*see p91*) in the **National Museum of the American Indian** (*see p85*).

AFTERNOON

Visit the **White House** (*see pp16–19*), then head south to the **Washington Monument** (*see p87*), then past the **Vietnam Veterans Memorial** (*see p86*) to the **Lincoln Memorial** (*see p86*) and **Jefferson Memorial** (*see p88*).

Day ❸

MORNING

Explore **Mount Vernon** (*see pp36–9*). Be sure to leave time to visit **George Washington's Distillery** (*see p63*).

AFTERNOON

Spend the afternoon at **Arlington National Cemetery** (*see pp34–5*). Head to **Old Town Alexandria** (*see p111*) for dinner.

Day ❹

MORNING

Early morning when the animals are active is the best time to explore the **National Zoo** (*see p112*). Then visit the **Washington National Cathedral** (*see pp30–31*) for a tour. Pause for lunch at **2amys** (*see p115*).

AFTERNOON

Head to **Georgetown** (*see pp104–7*), stopping to explore the gorgeous gardens at **Dumbarton Oaks**. Then a short walk leads to great shopping at **M Street and Wisconsin Avenue**. Finish with dinner at formal **1789** (*see p109*).

Top 10 Washington, DC Highlights

The US flag flying in front
of the United States Capitol

Washington, DC Highlights	10
United States Capitol	12
The White House	16
National Air and Space Museum	20
National Museum of American History	22
National Gallery of Art	24

National Museum of Natural History	28
Washington National Cathedral	30
National Museum of African American History and Culture	32
Arlington National Cemetery	34
Mount Vernon	36

TOP 10 Washington, DC Highlights

The political, cultural, and spiritual heart of the United States, Washington, DC dazzles its visitors with stirring icons, noble monuments, and magnificent museums at every turn. A selection of the best the city has to offer is explored in the following chapters.

US Capitol ①

The design of the US Capitol, with its iconic dome and Neo-Classical architecture, perfectly invokes the spirit of US democracy *(see pp12–15)*.

② The White House

The most elegant and familiar of all the world's political residences, the White House has witnessed some of the most consequential decisions of modern history *(see pp16–19)*.

③ National Air and Space Museum

Reportedly, this is the second most visited museum in the world. The artifacts within trace one of mankind's greatest quests *(see pp20–21)*.

National Museum of American History ④

This museum displays a mix of artifacts from "America's attic", ranging from political campaign buttons to historic examples of the Star-Spangled Banner *(see pp22–3)*.

⑤ National Gallery of Art

The National Gallery's vast collection makes it one of the greatest art museums in the world *(see pp24–7)*.

6 National Museum of Natural History

There are a lot of exhibits to explore from the famous Rotunda elephant to the fascinating Hope Diamond as well as the Insect Zoo, and the Butterfly Pavilion filled with live specimens *(see pp28–9)*.

7 Washington National Cathedral

Ancient and modern come together in this, the "national house of prayer," from the Gothic architecture to the Space Window *(see pp30–31)*.

8 National Museum of African American History and Culture

This museum chronicles the African American experience, tackling slavery, segregation, and civil rights. It also highlights Black cultural achievements *(see pp32–3)*.

10 Mount Vernon

George Washington's estate and mansion is a perfect example of the colonial plantations common in Virginia at the time of the Revolutionary War *(see pp36–9)*.

9 Arlington National Cemetery

Four million people each year visit these rolling lawns studded with the headstones of America's war dead. A moving and reflective experience *(see pp34–5)*.

🔟 ⭐ United States Capitol

From its elevated site, described as "a pedestal waiting for a monument," the Capitol has stood unwavering as the symbol of the American democractic process (an often rough-and-tumble one) throughout its more than 200-year history. The Capitol's frescoes and art collection qualify it as a notable museum, and eager visitors come to brush shoulders with history, both remembered and in the making.

US Capitol Floor plan

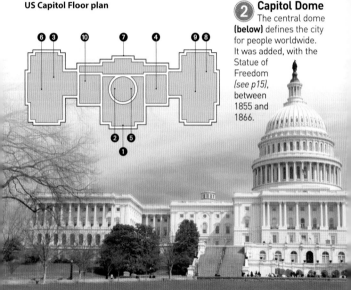

2 Capitol Dome
The central dome (below) defines the city for people worldwide. It was added, with the Statue of Freedom (see p15), between 1855 and 1866.

1 Capitol Visitor Center
The vast, underground Visitor Center (below) shows videos introducing Congress and the Capitol Complex, while the Exhibition Hall features displays and artifacts that recount the history of the Capitol.

3 Brumidi Corridors
Constantino Brumidi (1805–80) designed these ornate passage-ways on the lower floor of the Senate wing.

4 National Statuary Hall
The monumental *Liberty and the Eagle* by Enrico Causici (c.1819) overlooks this grand, semicircular hall. It was originally the House Chamber and now displays statues of histo-rical and political figures.

Columbus Doors 7

These imposing bronze doors **(right)**, 17 ft (5 m) tall, are made up of reliefs depicting Christopher Columbus's life and his arrival in America. Designed by Randolph Rogers, the doors were cast in Munich in 1860.

Hall of Columns 8

This striking corridor, more than 100 ft (30 m) long with lofty ceilings, is named after the 28 gracefully fluted white marble columns set along its length. It houses additional items from the collection of the original House Chamber.

Rotunda 5

America's first president ascends into the heavens in this 4,664-sq-ft- (430-sq-m-) fresco *The Apotheosis of Washington*, lining the interior of the monumental dome **(above)**.

Senate Chamber 6

A semicircle of 100 desks faces the dais in this eminent assembly room. Democrats sit to the right, while Republicans are seated to the left.

House Chamber 9

The largest room in the Capitol is used for daily deliberations of the House of Representatives and for joint meetings of the House and Senate.

Old Senate Chamber 10

Used by the Senate from 1810 to 1859, this fine chamber **(left)** has been the setting for crucial debates on core issues in the development of the United States.

NEED TO KNOW

MAP R5 ■ National Mall, between 1st and 3rd Sts and Constitution and Independence Aves, SW ■ 202-226-8000 ■ www. visitthecapitol.gov

Open 8:30am–4:30pm Mon–Sat; closed on Thanksgiving, Christmas, New Year's Day, and Inauguration Day

Advanced registration required for tours

....

■ The Visitor Center includes a restaurant, gift shop, and gathering place for tour groups. The Capitol Cafe is open 8:30am–4pm Mon–Sat.

■ Security protocols forbid certain items to be carried on tours, including liquids and aerosols, bulky bags, and all foods; check the website for details.

....

Capitol Guide
Guided tours (bookable via the official website) include historic areas of the Capitol, such as the Crypt, the Rotunda, and the National Statuary Hall. A separate pass is required to visit the galleries of the Senate and the House of Representatives which are open to the public when either legislative body is in session. Cameras, cell phones, and other recording devices are prohibited.

Events in the US Capitol's History

1 1791
George Washington selects the site for the new Capitol, with his city planner, Pierre Charles L'Enfant. They choose Jenkins Hill, 88 ft (27 m) above the north bank of the Potomac River.

2 1792
Dr. William Thornton wins a design contest for "Congress House," in which he proposed a simple central domed hall flanked by two rectangular wings.

3 1800
Congress moves from Philadelphia to occupy the north wing of the Capitol.

4 1811
The Capitol is fully occupied by the House of Representatives, Senate, Supreme Court, and Library of Congress.

5 1814
British troops occupy the city and burn many buildings, including the Capitol, during the War of 1812 (which lasted until 1815).

British burn the Capitol in the War of 1812

6 1818
Charles Bulfinch takes over the building's restoration and supervises its reconstruction. The Senate House and Supreme Court occupy new rooms by 1819, and the Rotunda is first used in 1824 to host a grand reception for General Lafayette.

George Washington

7 1851
The Capitol is again damaged by fire. It is rebuilt under Thomas U. Walter, who designs the cast-iron dome. Work continues on the Dome during the Civil War, while the Capitol is also used as a hospital, barracks, and bakery.

8 1880s–1900
Modern electrical lighting and the first elevator are installed. After another fire in 1898, fireproofing was at last added.

9 1958–1962
The east front is extended 32 ft (10 m) east of the old sandstone front. The west front is restored between 1983 and 1987. This work produces the Capitol we see today.

10 2021
The Capitol is stormed by the supporters of Donald Trump, attempting to overturn the result of the 2020 presidential election that was won by Joe Biden.

Illustration of the US Capitol in 1852

THE STATUE OF FREEDOM

Crowning the Capitol dome stands Thomas Crawford's *Statue of Freedom*, commissioned in 1855. Freedom is depicted as a classical female figure, draped in flowing robes. Her Roman helmet, however, features the crest of an eagle's head, feathers, and talons, which some believe to be a reference to American Indian dress. Crawford had originally substituted the Roman helmet for the liberty cap, a symbol of freeing formerly enslaved people, but the then US Secretary of War, Jefferson Davis, objected. The statue faces east in accordance with the front of the building, not, to the puzzlement of many visitors, towards the rest of the nation. The east front was made the main building entrance simply because it faces an approach of level ground. This monumental symbol of liberty is 19.5 ft (6 m) tall and weighs around 15,000 lbs (6,800 kg). Sadly Crawford died in 1857, before it was erected.

The American Ideal
The *Statue of Freedom* appears to face away from the heartland, but she is nevertheless supposed to be the embodiment of all Americans. She encapsulates the ideal of freedom for all citizens, as laid out in the US Constitution. It is an ideal that remains unfulfilled for many, and the struggle for "a more perfect Union" continues.

TOP 10
WORKS OF ART IN THE US CAPITOL

1 Statue of Freedom, Thomas Crawford (Dome)

2 The Apotheosis of Washington, Constantino Brumidi (Rotunda)

3 General George Washington Resigning His Commission, John Trumball (Rotunda)

4 Columbus Doors, Randolph Rogers (East Front)

5 Minton Tiles (floors and offices)

6 Brumidi Corridors (Senate Wing)

7 Portrait Monument to Lucretia Mott, Elizabeth Cady Stanton, and Susan B. Anthony, Adelaide Johnson (Rotunda)

8 Statuary (National Statuary Hall), Capitol Visitor Center, and other locations

9 Declaration of Independence, John Trumball (Rotunda)

10 Baptism of Pocahontas, prior to her marriage to John Rolfe, Antonio Cappellano (Rotunda)

TOP 10 ⭐ The White House

Possibly the most famous residential landmark in the world, this dramatic Neo-Classical mansion has been the residence of the US president and family, the seat of executive power, and a working office building for over 200 years. Situated at the nation's most recognizable address, 1600 Pennsylvania Avenue, the White House reflects the power of the presidency. Its 132 rooms preserve and display the cultural settings of America's past and present. Lafayette Park to the north and the Ellipse to the south are good sites for viewing this American icon.

1 North Facade
The stately but welcoming entrance on Pennsylvania Avenue **(below)** has a beautifully proportioned Ionic portico, added in 1829. Painted Virginia sandstone gives the building its white luster.

2 State Dining Room
As many as 140 guests may enjoy the president's hospitality in this formal dining room.

3 South Facade
The large semicircular portico **(right)** added in 1824 dominates the south view. The six main columns create an optical illusion, appearing to stretch from ground to roofline, emphasizing the classical proportions.

4 Map Room
Several graceful Chippendale pieces furnish this private meeting room. Franklin D. Roosevelt adapted it as his situation room to assess the progress of World War II.

5 East Room
The East Room has been used chiefly for large receptions and ceremonial gatherings, such as dances, award presentations, press conferences, banquets, and historic bill and treaty signings.

6 Blue Room
The Blue Room **(below)** is by far the most elegant of all the reception rooms – it was George Washington who suggested its oval shape.

7 Oval Office
Since 1909, this room **(left)** is the place for the president's core tasks. Leaders add their own touches – Barack Obama added a bust of Martin Luther King, Jr., and Joe Biden replaced a portrait of Andrew Jackson with one of Benjamin Franklin.

8 West Wing

This wing is the executive operational center of the White House. It was relocated here in 1902 to allow more privacy in the main building.

9 Lincoln Bedroom

Although the name for this room (below) is a misnomer – Abraham Lincoln actually used it as an office – a number of his possessions are on display here.

10 Visitor Center

The White House Visitor Center (below) has engrossing exhibits on various aspects of the mansion. It also offers park ranger talks, a souvenir shop, and special events such as military band concerts.

NEED TO KNOW

MAP N4 ◾ 1600 Pennsylvania Ave, NW
◾ 202-456-7041 (for information about tours)
◾ www.nps.gov/whho

Visitor Center: 1450 Pennsylvania Ave, NW

◾ If you have a telephoto lens or binoculars, the carved decorations on the Rose Garden and the north entrance, viewed from the Ellipse, deserve your attention.

◾ The White House has no public restrooms. The nearest facilities are at the Visitor Center and the Ellipse Visitor Pavilion, near 15th and E streets.

Touring the White House

If you want to tour the White House, you must start the process well before your visit. US citizens must request tickets from their Member of Congress. The request can be made up to three months in advance, but at the very minimum tickets must be requested 21 days in advance. Tickets are limited and issued on a first come, first served basis. Foreign visitors must make a request for tickets from their embassy in DC (though tickets for non-US residents are extremely difficult to come by).

These self-guided tours (subject to change) are available from 7:30am to 11:30am Tuesdays through Thursdays and 7:30am to 1:30pm Fridays and Saturdays (excluding federal holidays).

For more information, including a list of prohibited items, visit www.whitehouse.gov/about-the-white-house/tours-events/.

You can enjoy a virtual tour of the White House at the White House Visitor Center.

White House Decorative Features

The Diplomatic Reception Room

1 Diplomatic Reception Room Wallpaper

The panoramic wallpaper is a set of large "Views of North America" printed in France in 1834.

2 China Room Collection

The White House collection of china services had grown so large by 1917 that Mrs Woodrow Wilson set aside a room in which to display it. Today, state and family china belonging to nearly every US president fills the handsome display cabinets.

3 Lighter Relieving a Steamboat Aground

This 1847 painting in the Green Room, by George Caleb Bingham, conveys the vitality of the nation.

4 Library

This former storage room was turned into a library in 1935, and contains a collection of books intended to reflect the philosophical and practical aspects of the presidency. Many pieces of the furniture in this room are attributed to the cabinet-maker Duncan Phyfe.

5 Monroe Plateau

James Monroe ordered a gilt table service from France in 1817. The plateau centerpiece is an impressive 14.5 ft (4.5 m) long when fully extended.

6 Grand Staircase

Descending to the Central Hall on the north side, the Grand Staircase is used for ceremonial entrances to state events in the East Room. Portraits of 20th-century presidents line the stairwell.

7 The Vermeil Room

"Vermeil" refers to the collection of gilded objects by early 19th-century silversmiths on display. Portraits of several First Ladies adorn the walls, and the room is grounded by one of the Empire-style tables purchased by President Andrew Jackson in 1829 for use in the East Room.

Sand Dunes at Sunset, Atlantic City by Henry Ossawa Tanner

8 Sand Dunes at Sunset, Atlantic City

This beach landscape (c.1885) by Henry Ossawa Tanner was the first work by an African American to be hung in the White House.

9 North Entrance Carvings

Scottish stonemasons created the fine carved surround for the north doorway with flowing garlands of roses and acorns.

Elegant table in the Library

10 Seymour Tall-Case Clock

This Oval Office clock ticks so loudly that its pendulum must be stopped whenever any television broadcasts originate from the room.

PRESIDENT TRUMAN'S RENOVATIONS

Harry S. Truman

On moving into the White House, Harry S. Truman observed: "The floors pop and the drapes move back and forth," and "[t]he damned place is haunted, sure as shootin.'" In 1948, after investigation, engineers confirmed that it was structural weakness, not ghosts, that was causing the problems. Some people said the house was standing "only from force of habit." The only solution was to move the First Family out and completely rebuild the White House within its external walls, gutting the inside entirely, and building a steel frame within the shell. Within it, the building was recreated, room by room, from scratch. Most structural elements seen today were built between 1948 and 1952, although a few older elements had been carefully dismantled and re-installed during reconstruction. America's three major networks broadcast the first-ever television tour of the residence in 1952. President Truman himself proudly led the tour and even entertained viewers by playing a tune on one of the pianos in the East Room *(see p16)*. A decade later, the arbiter of style, Jacqueline Kennedy again restored many of the period features.

TOP 10
EVENTS IN THE WHITE HOUSE'S HISTORY

1 George Washington supervises construction (1792)

2 John and Abigail Adams move in (1800)

3 The Lewis and Clark expedition to the Northwest is planned (1803)

4 The British burn down the White House (1814)

5 James Monroe moves into the partially rebuilt residence (1817)

6 The Executive Mansion is renamed the "White House" (1901)

7 President Roosevelt's World War II "Fireside Chats" inform and inspire the American public

8 Jackie Kennedy restores the house (1961–2)

9 Richard Nixon announces his resignation (Aug 8, 1974)

10 Barack Obama becomes first African American President (2009)

The White House was gutted in 1948 and completely rebuilt.

TOP10 ★ National Air and Space Museum

This fascinating museum pays homage to some of the most ingenious and beautiful objects of flight, from the Wright brothers' biplane to powerful spacecraft. With thousands of artifacts that tell the story of aviation, planetary science, and space exploration the museum showcases historic objects that reflect the American spirit of courage and innovation.

1 Moving Beyond Earth

This exhibition **(below)** explores the history of human spaceflight in the US during the Space Shuttle and International Space Station era, interpreting the story of human spaceflight through artifacts, immersive experiences, and high-tech interactive kiosks.

2 1903 Wright Flyer

On December 17, 1903, Orville Wright flew this twin-winged craft **(left)** 120 ft (35 m), making it the first powered, piloted plane to be airborne. Muslin on a spruce and ash frame provided a light but strong body. The Wright brothers also designed the engine.

3 How Things Fly

Hands-on exhibits here lead visitors through the basics of flight, both human and animal, and explain forces that control flight of all types, from a helium balloon to a mission to Mars.

4 Neil Armstrong's Apollo 11 Spacesuit

Efforts were made to preserve the space-suit **(above)** that Neil Armstrong wore when he walked on the Moon.

5 Skylab Orbital Workshop

This gold cylinder was an identical backup to the workshop module that provided living and research space for the first US space station.

6 Boeing Milestones of Flight Hall

The soaring "Boeing Milestones of Flight" gallery highlights major firsts in aviation and space travel, including the groundbreaking SpaceShipOne.

7 Time and Navigation

This fascinating exhibit documents the evolution of timekeeping, from navigating the oceans to tracking our location using orbiting satellites, and how it has influenced how we find our way.

Museum Floor plan

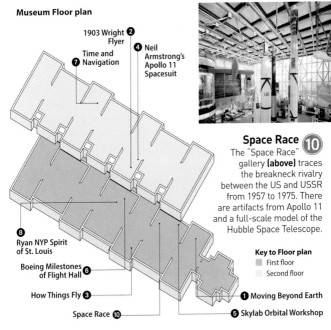

1903 Wright Flyer **2**

Time and Navigation **7**

Neil Armstrong's Apollo 11 Spacesuit **4**

Space Race **10**

The "Space Race" gallery **(above)** traces the breakneck rivalry between the US and USSR from 1957 to 1975. There are artifacts from Apollo 11 and a full-scale model of the Hubble Space Telescope.

8 Ryan NYP Spirit of St. Louis

Boeing Milestones of Flight Hall **6**

How Things Fly **3**

Space Race **10**

Key to Floor plan
First floor
Second floor

1 Moving Beyond Earth

5 Skylab Orbital Workshop

8 Ryan NYP Spirit of St. Louis

In 1927, Charles Lindbergh flew this plane on the world's first solo transatlantic flight, 3,610 miles (5,810 km) from Long Island to Paris. His 33-hour flight made him one of the most famous men of his age. The initials NYP in the plane's name stand for New York–Paris.

9 Steven F. Udvar-Hazy Center

Located 30 miles (48 km) away from the main museum site, this display and restoration center consists of two exhibition hangars near Dulles Airport. Opened to celebrate the 100th anniversary of the Wright brothers' first powered flight, it has nearly 300 aircraft and spacecraft, including the space shuttle *Discovery*.

NEED TO KNOW

MAP Q5 ▪ Jefferson Drive between 4th & 7th St, SW ▪ 202-633-2214 ▪ www. airandspace.si.edu

Open 10am–5:30pm daily; closed Dec 25

Adm required only for theater screenings: $9 adults, $8 seniors, $7.50 children (2–12 years), $6.50 for members of the Smithsonian

Steven F. Udvar-Hazy Center: 14390 Air and Space Museum Pkwy, Chantilly, VA 20151; 703-572-4118; open 10am–5:30pm daily

▪ Flight Line Café is on the first floor of the Mall building and there's a full-service McDonald's at Steven F. Udvar-Hazy Center.

▪ The World War II display at the Udvar-Hazy Center features the "Enola Gay"– the first aircraft to drop an atomic bomb.

Museum Guide

The museum will be undergoing a large-scale renovation until late 2025, but will remain open with phased closures and openings (check website for details). During this time, the entrance will be on Jefferson Drive, which leads into Boeing Milestones of Flight Hall with the Welcome Center. To see a film at the Lockheed Martin IMAX Theater, buy tickets on arrival, or in advance online.

TOP 10 ⭐ National Museum of American History

Three huge floors filled with a variety of fascinating objects make up this paean to American culture. The first floor focuses on science and technology, including hands-on experiments and exhibitions on transport, electricity, and machinery. The second floor is home to the famous Star-Spangled Banner, while the third floor features a stirring tribute to the American presidency and military history.

1 The Price of Freedom: Americans at War
This gallery explores the nation's military history, from the French and Indian War in the 1750s to recent conflicts in Afghanistan and Iraq.

2 Ruby Slippers
Dorothy's famous ruby slippers from the iconic 1939 movie *The Wizard of Oz*, have a new home in a gallery meant to evoke the Technicolor world of the Emerald City. This popular artifact is back on view following a conservation treatment.

3 Ray Dolby Gateway to Culture
With a series of eight installations based on sound, stadium and screen, this gallery focuses on exploring American history through culture, arts and entertainment. Exhibits and displays include the landmark stained-glass window, the Hall of Music, Graham Bell's graphophone and the Ruby Slippers among others.

4 The First Ladies
The First Ladies' gallery includes inaugural gowns worn by Jackie Kennedy, Nancy Reagan, Frances Cleveland **(left)**, Michelle Obama, and many others.

5 FOOD: Transforming the American Table 1950–2000
American chef Julia Child's actual kitchen **(above)** opens this exploration of the significant changes in the production and consumption of food and wine in postwar America.

6 American Enterprise
This exhibition chronicles the interaction between capitalism and democracy that resulted in the constant evolution of the American market. Visitors are taken on a journey through interactive displays and an ever-growing list of collected objects to experience the country's growth as one of the most vibrant economies.

🔟 Within These Walls...

A two-story colonial Massachusetts house has been rebuilt in the museum, to explore the 200-year-long history of the families who lived and worked there.

7️⃣ The Star-Spangled Banner

The flag that inspired the national anthem (above) is strikingly large – originally 30 by 42 ft (9 by 13 m) – although timeworn. Made by Baltimore flag-maker Mary Pickersgill in 1813, it is in a gallery that re-creates the Battle of Baltimore and the burning of the White House.

8️⃣ Greensboro Lunch Counter

This is a small section of the actual lunch counter in a Woolworth store in Greensboro, where African American college students protested segregation in 1960.

Museum Floor plan
Key to Floor plan
- ◼ First floor
- ◼ Second floor
- ◼ Third floor

2️⃣ Ruby Slippers
4️⃣ The First Ladies
Ray Dolby 3️⃣ Gateway to Culture
The Price of Freedom 1️⃣
Greensboro 8️⃣ Lunch Counter
Within 🔟 These Walls
The Star- 7️⃣ Spangled Banner
American 6️⃣ Enterprise
9️⃣ The American Presidency
5️⃣ FOOD

9️⃣ The American Presidency

Highlights include George Washington's military uniform, and the top hat (above) Lincoln was wearing the night he was assassinated.

NEED TO KNOW

MAP P4 ◼ 14th St and Constitution Ave, NW ◼ 202-633-1000 ◼ www.americanhistory.si.edu

Open 10am–5:30pm daily; extended hours in summer (check on the website); closed Dec 25

◼ The Eat at America's Table and LeRoy Neiman Jazz Café are both located within the museum and offer a variety of dishes.

Museum Events
An amazing variety of events, both entertaining and enlightening, are available to the public. Phone ahead or check online for updates. Try out some of the interactive exhibits, or take part in debates on controversial issues. The museum hosts regular performances of the Smithsonian Jazz Masterworks Orchestra and Smithsonian Chamber Music Society. Important anniversaries are also marked by special events, talks, lectures, and discussions.

🔟 ⭐ National Gallery of Art

The collections at this immense gallery rival those of any art museum in the world, displaying milestones of Western art from the Middle Ages to the 21st century and including Italian Renaissance works, Dutch Masters, French Impressionists, and all ages of American art. John Russell Pope designed the harmonious Neo-Classical West Building in 1941.

4 The Adoration of the Magi

This festive view of the Magi at Christ's birthplace **(left)** was painted in tempura on a circular panel by Fra Angelico and Fra Filippo Lippi in about 1445.

5 Watson and the Shark

The dramatic subject matter, muscular painting, and expressions of dread and anxiety meant that this John Singleton Copley painting caused a sensation when it was first displayed in 1778.

1 Alexander Calder

The largest collection of Alexander Calder's works is housed here, with numerous vivid paintings and sculptures spanning from the late 1920s to 1976.

3 Ginevra de' Benci

The modeling of lustrous flesh against juniper make this Leonardo canvas of 1474 – his only one in the Americas – a lively, composed work.

2 The Jolly Flatboatmen

George Caleb Bingham's 1846 masterpiece **(below)** is a realistic depiction of life and work along one of America's largest rivers.

6 Girl with the Red Hat

This 1665 portrait **(above)** shows off Johannes Vermeer's striking use of color: yellow highlights in the blue robe, purple under the hat, turquoise in the eyes. The luminosity is enhanced by the smooth panel base.

9 The River of Light

Frederick Edwin Church's 1877 oil painting of the Amazon is based on sketches taken during a trip to South America. This otherworldly work emphasizes the power of nature.

7 Right and Left

The title of Winslow Homer's 1909 work (above) refers to shooting ducks with separate barrels of a shotgun. The fleeting nature of the ducks' existence echoes our own.

Museum Floor plan, West Building

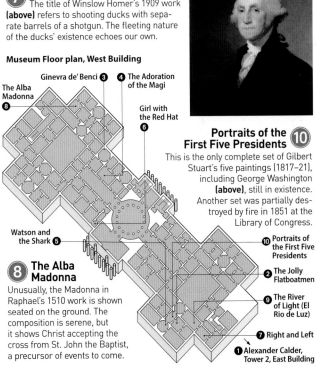

Ginevra de' Benci **3** — **4** The Adoration of the Magi

The Alba Madonna **8**

Girl with the Red Hat **6**

Watson and the Shark **5**

10 Portraits of the First Five Presidents

This is the only complete set of Gilbert Stuart's five paintings (1817–21), including George Washington (above), still in existence. Another set was partially destroyed by fire in 1851 at the Library of Congress.

10 Portraits of the First Five Presidents

2 The Jolly Flatboatmen

9 The River of Light (El Rio de Luz)

7 Right and Left

1 Alexander Calder, Tower 2, East Building

8 The Alba Madonna

Unusually, the Madonna in Raphael's 1510 work is shown seated on the ground. The composition is serene, but it shows Christ accepting the cross from St. John the Baptist, a precursor of events to come.

NEED TO KNOW

MAP Q4 ■ 3rd–9th Sts at Constitution Ave, NW ■ 202-737-4215 ■ www.nga.gov

Open 10am–5pm daily; closed Dec 25, Jan 1

■ Pick up an interactive guide at the Education Studio in the East Building for a list of places to eat, hands-on activities, plus story times and other family-friendly programs.

■ The gallery acquired over 8,000 works from the world-renowned Corcoran Gallery of Art, which closed in 2014. Many of these are now on display in the West Building.

Gallery Guide

The main floor contains European paintings and sculpture and American art. The ground floor has works on paper, sculpture, decorative arts, and temporary exhibits. An underground concourse leads to the East Building, which has modern works from the late 19th century to the present day.

National Gallery of Art Collections

The Dance Lesson, a 19th-century Impressionist painting by Edgar Degas

1 French 19th-Century Paintings

Especially rich in Impressionist works, this collection includes some of the world's most beloved works of art, such as Monet's *Japanese Footbridge* and Degas' *Four Dancers* and *The Dance Lesson*.

2 American Paintings

The breadth of this collection reveals many interesting themes: portraiture, a desire for accuracy in depicting American life and landscape, and a social conscience.

3 Italian 13th- to 16th-Century Paintings

Best known for the increasing mastery of the naturalistic portrayal of the human figure and of interior and exterior settings, the works in this extensive collection still have appealing variety: decorative, mystical, simple, and elegant.

4 Italian, French, and Spanish 16th-Century Paintings

The mature flowering of the Renaissance bursts forth in this broad collection of works by Raphael, Giorgione, Titian, and many others.

5 Photographs and Drawings

Repeat visitors see an almost unbelievable quantity and variety of exquisite drawings, prints, illustrated books, and photographs. The permanent collection contains more than 65,000 items, dating as far back as the 11th century.

6 17th-Century Dutch and Flemish Paintings

Visitors will find an overwhelmingly rich array of Old Master works by artists such as Rembrandt, Frans Hals, Van Dyck, Rubens, Vermeer, and their contemporaries.

7 Spanish Paintings

El Greco, Zurbarán, Murillo, and Velázquez are just some of the 18th- to 19th-century highlights in this vibrant collection.

8 Decorative Arts

Sumptuous tapestries, full of imagery, outstanding pieces of furniture, and everyday items such as Chinese porcelain plates and bowls, give a wonderful glimpse of passing centuries.

Collections Floor plan

Key to Floor plan
- Ground floor
- Main floor

9 European Sculpture

Portrait busts and portrait medals have always been important products of the sculptor's studio, and many fine examples are displayed here. There is also an especially absorbing selection of Rodin's work and some interesting experimental sculptural pieces by Degas.

10 Painting and Sculpture of the 20th Century

In the East Building you can trace the frantic rate of change in 20th-century art, from Matisse's Fauvist works, the Cubists Picasso and Braque, the abstraction of Mondrian, and Surrealists such as Magritte and Miró right up to Minimalism and Pop Art.

THE EAST BUILDING AND SCULPTURE GARDEN

The East Building is an angular construction designed to house permanent and touring exhibitions of contemporary art. Its entrance is from 4th Street or from the underground concourse leading from the West Building. In the upper level of the East Building is Jackson Pollock's masterpiece, Number One, 1950 (Lavender Mist). If you look closely at the upper left-hand corner of the canvas, you'll find the abstract impressionist's handprints. The new fourth floor features an outdoor sculpture terrace and two skylit gallery towers. The Sculpture Garden is a lively public space integrating contemporary art with beautifully landscaped gardens and a relaxing reflection pool with its spraying central fountain. In a 6-acre- (2.5-ha-) block next to the West Building, the garden has native trees, shrubs, and perennials, along with 21 pieces from the gallery's collection and several items here on loan from other museums. There are free jazz concerts on summer Fridays, and the pool transforms into a popular ice-skating rink in winter.

The magnificent East Building

TOP 10
WORKS IN THE SCULPTURE GARDEN

1 Moondog, Tony Smith (1964–99)

2 Personnage Gothique, Oiseau-Éclair, Joan Miró (1974)

3 Six-Part Seating, Scott Burton (1985–98)

4 Puellae (Girls), Magdalena Abakanowicz (1992)

5 Chair Transformation Number 20B, Lucas Samaras (1996)

6 House I, Roy Lichtenstein (1996–8)

7 Spider, Louise Bourgeois (1996)

8 Four-Sided Pyramid, Sol LeWitt (1997)

9 Thinker on a Rock, Barry Flanagan (1997)

10 Graft, Roxy Paine (2008)

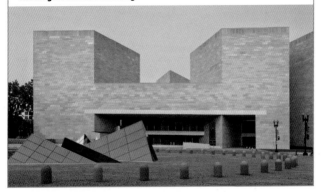

TOP 10 ⭐ National Museum of Natural History

From the earrings of Marie Antoinette to the giant jaws of a prehistoric shark, this museum is full of fascinating treasures collected by Smithsonian scientists for over a century. Ancient mummies, rare gems and minerals, previously unknown plants and animals, and the bones of mighty dinosaurs are on display, making this one of the most popular museums on the Mall.

5 African Elephant
This huge bull elephant (left) seems to fill the Rotunda and has become a symbol of the museum itself. Weighing in at over 8 tons, this was the largest land animal on display when it was unveiled in 1959. Exhibits tell the story of African elephants and the threats they face today.

3 Fossil Lab
Look through the windows into a genuine fossil lab where museum scientists clean, prepare, and mount fossils from around the world that have recently been collected by scientists.

6 African Voices
The exhibits in this section explore African art, political activism, and community life – charting the worldwide influence of Africa's peoples and cultures over time.

1 Hope Diamond
Not the world's largest diamond, but certainly the most famous, and possibly the most viewed artifact in any museum in the world. The 45.52 carat deep-blue diamond (left) was part of the French Crown Jewels, and is reputed to be cursed.

2 The Last American Dinosaur
The museum's legendary National Fossil Hall reopened in mid-2019. Visitors can view this special exhibit that highlights the lives of large dinosaurs that roamed the earth just before a global catastrophe (a massive asteroid) ended their reign.

4 Hall of Mammals
From a roaring African lion (above) to an enormous Grizzly Bear standing on its hind legs, this hall is filled with dramatic representations of warm-blooded animals from around the world.

8 Live Butterfly Pavilion

A family favorite, this pavilion lets you stroll among fluttering beauties with fanciful names like Gulf Fritillary **(left)** and Madagascar Moon Moth.

7 Ptolemaic Mummy

This mummy of a 40-year-old man who died over 2,000 years ago is the star of "Eternal Life in Ancient Egypt." Displays include a step-by-step guide to the process of mummification.

Museum Floor plan

Fossil Lab ❸
❷ The Last American Dinosaur
Ptolemaic Mummy ❼
❶ Hope Diamond
Live Butterfly Pavilion ❽
❾ Giant Squid
❻ African Voices
Hall of Mammals ❹
Key to Floor plan
▨ Ground floor
▨ First floor
▨ Second floor
❺ African Elephant
❿ Neanderthal Man

ORIGINS OF THE SMITHSONIAN

The world's largest museum complex, the Smithsonian Institute was founded in 1826 when British scientist James Smithson left half a million dollars (about $15 million today) "to found in Washington, under the name of the Smithsonian Institution, an establishment for the increase and diffusion of knowledge among men." Today, the Smithsonian Institute in Washington comprises 19 museums, 9 research centers, and a zoo, and every one of its public venues can be entered free of charge.

9 Giant Squid

The Sant Ocean Hall features a 25-ft- (7.6-m-) female giant squid, found on the coast of Spain in 2005. The larger of the two specimens is displayed here.

10 Neanderthal Man

The result of painstaking forensic and reconstruction work, this life-size head is one of many artifacts exploring the evolution of humans.

NEED TO KNOW

MAP P4 ▪ 10th St and Constitution Ave, NW ▪ 202-633-1000 ▪ www.naturalhistory.si.edu

Open 10am–5:30pm daily; closed Dec 25

Adm by timed ticket to the Live Butterfly Pavilion; book online

▪ The Atrium Café offers locally sourced vegetables and hormone-free meats, in the form of burgers, pizzas, deli sandwiches, and other family-pleasing meals. Ocean Terrace Café offers coffee drinks, ice cream, and desserts.

▪ Teens, tweens, and children will enjoy Q?rius (pronounced "curious"), an interactive learning space connecting science with everyday life and offering young people a new way to discover the natural world. Q?rius features real museum objects and artifacts. Visit qrius.si.edu for opening hours.

▪ If you want a quieter museum experience, it's a good idea to plan on visiting from Monday to Wednesday. Saturday is usually the busiest day of the week.

TOP 10 ⭐ Washington National Cathedral

This Gothic building is the focus of public spiritual life. The sixth largest cathedral in the world, it was completed in 1990, with a 10-story-high nave and a central tower 301 ft (92 m) tall, the highest point in the District of Columbia. This Episcopal church is officially named the Cathedral Church of Saint Peter and Saint Paul.

6 Main Entrance and Creation

The west entrance is centered within a high Gothic arch containing a lovely rose window. Sited above the huge bronze double doors is *Ex Nihilo*, a relief by 20th-century American sculptor Frederick Hart, which portrays the creation of humankind from chaos.

1 Creation Rose Window

This remarkably beautiful stained-glass window **(right)** celebrates the majesty and mystery of creation. It includes every color the artists – designed by Rowan LeCompte and created by Dieter Goldkuhle – could produce.

2 Space Window

This stained-glass window by artist Rodney Winfield is notable for commemorating mankind's 20th-century moon landing. A piece of moon rock, brought back by Apollo 11 astronauts, is embedded in it.

3 Exterior

The architecture of the cathedral is predominantly English Gothic, created using authentic methods dating from the Middle Ages, including a cross-shaped floorplan, flying buttresses, and spired towers **(right)**.

4 Pipe Organ

This magnificent Aeolian-Skinner instrument has 10,647 pipes. On most Mondays and Wednesdays at 12:30pm, an organist gives visitors a presentation and then demonstrates with a mini-recital.

5 Nave

The vertical impression given by the nave **(left)** is also typical of English Gothic style. Flags of the states are often displayed around the outer walls.

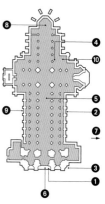

Cathedral Floor plan

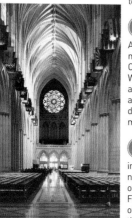

⑦ Gardens

A medieval walled garden is the model for the cathedral's beautiful Bishop's Garden **(right)** on the south side of the church. The herb gardens are a delight to the nose as well as the eye. All the stones here originated in a quarry that George Washington once owned.

BUILDING THE CATHEDRAL

In 1893, Congress granted a charter to construct Washington National Cathedral. Theodore Roosevelt attended the laying of the foundation stone at the Mount St. Albans location in 1907. The stone was brought from a field near Bethlehem. The completion of the west towers in 1990 marked the end of 83 years of ceaseless work. In 2011, the cathedral was severely damaged by an earthquake and works to restore the structure continue.

⑧ High Altar

The imposing high altar at the east end of the magnificent nave is made from stone dug from Solomon's quarry outside Jerusalem.

⑨ Gargoyles and Grotesques

Derived from decorated spouts on European buildings, the Cathedral is protected by some 1,242 carved grotesques, including 112 working gargoyles, as well as Darth Vader.

⑩ Children's Chapel

This endearing room is child-scaled, with a miniature organ and altar and chairs to fit six-year-olds. Jesus is shown as a boy in the sculpture here. An exhibit here aims to build the world's largest LEGO Cathedral.

NEED TO KNOW

MAP H4 ▪ 3101 Wisconsin Aves, NW ▪ 202-537-6200
▪ www.cathedral.org

Open 10am–5:30pm Mon–Fri, 10am–4pm Sat, 12:45am–4pm Sun (weekend hours subject to change); worship at 8am; tours begin at 12:45

Adm $12 adults; $8 senior citizens & youth 5–17yrs; free under 5 yrs; free for services and worship & on Sun

▪ The cathedral offers live music concerts year-round.

▪ Use binoculars to see the gargoyles and grotesques.

TOP 10 ⭐ National Museum of African American History and Culture

This enlightening museum traces African American history from the roots of slavery to the election of the US's first African American president and beyond. There are also memorabilia and artifacts highlighting African American contributions to sports, music, visual arts, and the US military.

Taking the Stage ③

This gallery **(right)**, on Level 4, charts the history of African Americans in theater, film, and television, focusing on how Black artists have challenged racial discrimination and stereotypes in cinema.

① Emmett Till Memorial

This poignant memorial **(above)** commemorates the murder of Emmett Till in 1955. His brutal lynching, and the acquittal of his killers, helped spark the civil rights movement.

④ Harriet Tubman's Shawl

In the "Slavery and Freedom" exhibition, visitors can see Harriet Tubman's silk lace and linen shawl – a gift given by Queen Victoria to the famous abolitionist and Underground Railroad "conductor."

THE BUILDING: A SHINING SYMBOL

This museum dominates its section at the National Mall. Its striking shape and contemporary structure stand in contrast to the older Neo-Classical buildings. Designed by Ghanaian British architect David Adjaye, the building took around four years to complete. The three-tiered metallic facade of the structure is covered in 3,600 bronze cast-aluminum panels forming an intricate lattice, which symbolize the African Americans striving to rise upward.

② The Contemplative Court

Light filters through an Oculus skylight down to this underground exhibition **(above)**. Visitors can pause at this tranquil space and read inspirational quotes from Nelson Mandela and other Black leaders.

5 A Changing America: 1968 and Beyond

This exhibition on Concourse 1 chronicles the history of Black America from the assassination of Martin Luther King, Jr. and the Black Power movement in the late 1960s and 1970s, to the re-election of President Barack Obama in 2012.

9 Join the Step Show

This interactive show introduces the African American dance form of stepping (using footsteps, claps, and spoken words). Visitors can also practice moves with members of the dance group Step Afrika!, the first ever professional company dedicated to stepping.

It's a thing been happening to me all my life.

6 Musical Crossroads

A fascinating exhibition, which explores the influence of African American music on mainstream American culture.

7 Follow the Green Book

This interactive car exhibit uses Victor H. Green's guide to illustrate Jim Crow-era travel challenges for African Americans.

Sports: Leveling the Playing Field 8

This exhibition explores the political role that sports have played in African American culture, including the Black Power salute **(right)** at the 1968 Olympics.

10 Oprah Winfrey Theater

Named after the famous TV personality Oprah Winfrey, this 350-seat, state-of-the-art theater screens films, such as Ava Duvernay's *August 28*, throughout the day. Check the website for details.

NEED TO KNOW

MAP P4 ▪ 1400 Constitution Ave, NW ▪ 844-750-3012 ▪ www.nmaahc.si.edu

Open 10am–5:30pm daily; closed Dec 25

▪ The museum is free, but it is so popular that timed-entry passes are required. Check the website for advance tickets. During off-peak times visitors can enter the museum on week-days without passes.

▪ The Sweet Home Café, on the Concourse level, specializes in African American cuisine and soul food.

Gallery Guide

There are eight levels in the museum, four above ground and four below. The main entrances – the National Mall and Constitution Avenue – lead to Heritage Hall on Level 1 where the information and ticket desks are located. Below is the Concourse level, which has the Contemplative Court and the Oprah Winfrey Theater. The museum's underground galleries display exhibits on slavery and segregation, while the higher, brighter floors focus on emancipation and civil rights. Start with the lowest level of the History Galleries on C3, before moving up to C2, and then finally to C1.

Level 2 has the "Explore More!" interactive galleries, while Level 3 features the Community Galleries. Level 4 has the Culture Galleries that focus on music and the arts.

TOP 10 ⭐ Arlington National Cemetery

The nation's best-known military cemetery, the rolling lawns of the Arlington National Cemetery are filled with white headstones, the Tomb of the Unknown Soldier, and the grave of President John F. Kennedy – the visible symbols of sacrifices made for freedom. The flags fly at half-staff before the first and after the last of 25–27 funerals per weekday, as the cemetery continues to honor the graves of veterans. More than three million people visit every year.

Lawns of Graves ①

More than 400,000 people are buried on these grounds, marked by simple graves, arranged in regular grids, spread across the lawns **(right)**. Although only a small percentage of America's war dead lie here, the expanse gives a tangible picture of the human cost of war.

⑥ Memorial Amphitheater

This marble amphitheater **(left)** is the setting for the Memorial Day (see p73), Easter sunrise service, and Veterans Day ceremonies, when the nation's leaders pay tribute to those who have served their country.

② Tuskegee Airmen Memorial Tree and Plaque

This plaque is dedicated to the 84 Tuskegee Airmen who lost their lives in World War II.

③ Pierre L'Enfant Monument

Honoring the designer of the Washington city grid (see p42), L'Enfant's monument shows his magnificent plan of the city within a circle.

④ Arlington House

Lee's mansion was actually conceived as a memorial to George Washington, built by his adopted grandson.

⑤ Tomb of the Unknown Soldier

This monument **(right)** is guarded 24 hours a day by the 3rd U.S. Infantry Regiment (Old Guard). Unknown soldiers of World Wars I and II and the Korean War lie here.

9 Rough Riders Monument

This granite monument **(left)** displays the insignia of the First US Volunteer Cavalry (the "Rough Riders") and the battles they fought during the Spanish–American War.

CIVIL WAR ORIGINS

Robert E. Lee lived in Arlington House until 1861, when tensions between the Union and the Southern states reached a crisis. When Virginia seceded from the Union and joined the Confederacy, Lee became a general of Virginia's military forces. Union troops then crossed the Potomac and took possession of Arlington House. In 1864, Arlington National Cemetery was created to cope with the mass deaths of the Civil War.

7 Seabees Memorial

A bronze construction worker pauses to help a child. The Seabees (members of Naval Construction Battalions) performed daring feats in building the military bases needed to win World War II.

8 Space Shuttle Memorials

One memorial honors the astronauts who died in the space shuttle *Challenger* disaster in 1986. Another nearby is to the crew lost in the 2003 *Columbia* shuttle tragedy.

10 President John F. Kennedy Gravesite

The eternal flame next to the grave **(above)** of the assassinated president was lit by the then first lady Jacqueline Kennedy on the day of his funeral.

Map of the Cemetery

NEED TO KNOW

MAP K6 ■ Arlington, VA ■ 877-907-8585

Open Apr–Sep: 8am–7pm daily; Oct–Mar: to 5pm daily ■ www.arlingtoncemetery.mil

■ The ANC tour bus departs from the Welcome Center and stops at major sites. Tickets cost $17.95 for adults, $9.95 for children (4–12), $13.95 for seniors (65 years and over), $7.95 for active duty military (plus four family members), free for active duty military in uniform, free shuttles to gravesite.

■ The Welcome Center has a bookstore, restrooms, and water fountains.

TOP 10 ★ Mount Vernon

At the age of 22, George Washington began running this mansion on the banks of the Potomac River. Mount Vernon remained both his and his wife Martha's home for the next 45 years, and offers an insight into his character and life. Alongside this, the mansion's role as part of Virginia's slavery-based plantation society is covered here. The lives of the over 500 enslaved persons who built and maintained the mansion are a key part of this story.

6 Chintz Room

Nelly Custis, Martha Washington's granddaughter, lived here from early childhood. This richly furnished bedchamber was hers; she was likely attended here by Molly, one of the enslaved housemaids.

1 Mansion's Exterior

The huge "piazza" or porch **(above)** overlooking the Potomac was the president's own design, though it was built by his enslaved labor force. The house is made of yellow pine, but the exterior was "rusticated" with a treatment that recreates the look of weathered stone.

2 Little Parlor

This pretty room reflects the informal family life of the house, and was especially set aside for music. The original harpsichord Washington purchased for Nelly Custis, is displayed in the museum.

3 New Room

This impressive room **(right)** was designed to be a grand "salon" in 18th-century English style. Washington used it as a formal area to receive visitors, as an art gallery, and occasionally for dining.

4 Washington's Bedchamber

Washington's spacious bedroom was primarily Martha's sanctuary, where she planned her day and wrote letters. She was attended by her enslaved lady's maids, Ona "Oney" Judge, and later (after Judge liberated herself), Caroline Branham.

5 Front Parlor

This charming parlor was one of George Washington's favorite rooms **(right)**, and he had it decorated in stylish cream paint, with stunning blue period furniture. Tea and coffee were served here. Ten enslaved waiters and housemaids, including butler Frank Lee, served the family at the mansion.

9 Kitchen
The mansion's enslaved cooks, Doll, Hercules, Nathan, and Lucy, got up at 4am each morning to prepare daily meals here **(left)** – all the fuel and water had to be hauled in by hand. They planned the menus under Martha's supervision.

7 Lafayette Bedchamber
The Marquis de Lafayette, one of Washington's military aides and a lifelong friend, is thought to have stayed in this guest bedroom with a breathtaking view of the Potomac.

10 Study
This room was the setting for Washington's commercial, political, and public work. It was also his dressing room, and was most probably attended by his enslaved valets William Lee and Christopher Sheels.

BUILDING MOUNT VERNON

George Washington's great-grandfather acquired the Mount Vernon estate in 1674 as a tobacco plantation. The original house was built around 1734 for George's father Augustine. George started leasing the estate in 1754 and formally inherited it seven years later. He then expanded the mansion and grounds with the help of enslaved labor.

NEED TO KNOW

3200 Mount Vernon Memorial Highway, VA ▪ 703-780-2000 ▪ www.mountvernon.org

Open Apr–Oct: 9am–5pm daily; Nov–Mar: 9am–4pm daily

Adm $28 adults; $15 children 6–11 years; free under 6 yrs; discount on tickets online

▪ Special events and outdoor concerts are held throughout the year. Check website for details and dates.

▪ The Mount Vernon shops sell seeds of some of the estate's heritage plants, as well as gardening books detailing their care.

▪ Outside the main entrance is a complex with a full-service restaurant, the Mount Vernon Inn, which offers specialties such as peanut and chestnut soup and salmon corncakes, as well as a food court which serves snacks and quick eats.

Mount Vernon Floor plan

Key to Floor plan
▪ First floor
▪ Second floor
▪ Third floor

8 Cupola
The cupola, with its "dove-of-peace" weathervane, provides light to the third floor and aids air circulation in summer.

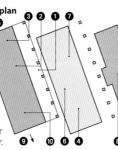

Mount Vernon Grounds

The reconstructed 16-sided treading barn in Mount Vernon Grounds

1 16-Sided Treading Barn
Open Apr–Oct

With this unique design, George Washington created aesthetically pleasing and efficient working barns. The building's circular plan with its slatted upper floor allowed horses to tread over grain placed on the floor, which separated the heads from the stalks. The grain then fell through the slats into temporary storage below. The building seen today is a reconstruction of the original based on thorough research by numerous archaeologists and curators.

The Mount Vernon wharf

2 Shipping and Receiving Dock

The wharf of the plantation was the main transportation center for shipping outbound produce and receiving farming and household supplies. The Potomac River was a major carrier of passengers and trade goods in Washington's day. At this evocative spot on its banks, it is easy to imagine the bustle and excitement of early commerce on the Potomac River.

3 River Tours
City Experiences: 800-459-8105; www.cityexperiences.com
■ **Open Apr–Oct**

Visitors can still use the Potomac River to reach Mount Vernon. The City Experiences tour boat line serves the wharf from the city: boats usually depart DC at 9:30am and return at 2pm. The tour operator has a ticket option that includes entry to Mount Vernon. Check the website for details.

4 Slave Quarters

Those who were enslaved lived in rough log cabins in small "villages" distributed across the estate so that they were conveniently close to the farms they were assigned. In his will, Washington freed all his enslaved workers. However, this only applied to 123 of the total 317 in bondage at Mount Vernon at his death. By law, enslaved persons owned by Martha Washington's estate (from her first husband Daniel Parke Custis) were inherited by the Custis grandchildren.

5 Washington's Tomb

This tomb is the second to hold the remains of George and Martha Washington. It was erected in 1831 based on Washington's own instructions and, in the years since, the tomb has been visited by millions of people who come to pay their respects to the first US president.

6 Upper and Lower Gardens

The wonderfully colorful upper flower garden is densely planted with varieties known to be cultivated in Washington's time. The lower garden was primarily worked by enslaved people under the direction of Martha Washington. This expansive plot yielded a wealth of vegetables and berries for the plantation's kitchens.

7 The Greenhouse

The handsome greenhouse complex once helped protect exotic and valuable plants through the cold Virginian winter. Revolutionary-War-era visitors to Mount Vernon could enjoy English grapes, lemons, limes, and oranges, as well as a host of flowering tropical plants.

8 Museum

Over 700 artifacts offer an in-depth look at Washington's life and career from his early days as a surveyor to his post-presidency days at Mount Vernon. Among the items on display are his dress sword and his field bed from the Revolutionary War. The museum also tackles slavery at Mount Vernon, with exhibits on the food, clothing, and housing of the enslaved people.

George Washington's whiskey distillery

9 Gristmill and Distillery
Route 235 S ▪ Open Apr–Oct: 10am–5pm daily

Located 2.7 miles (4.3 km) west of the estate is Washington's 18th-century watermill, which played an important part in his vision for America as a "granary to the world." Today, millers in colonial costume grind wheat into flour and corn meal just as was done in the 1700s. Archaeologists excavated the site of Washington's 1797 whiskey distillery, and a fully reconstructed distillery now provides demonstrations and hands-on activities for visitors.

10 Pioneer Farm

George Washington was passionate about improving the agricultural methods of his time. The Pioneer Farm showcases many new ideas and techniques he worked with, including a redesigned plow, crop rotation, and even organic farming. It also offers visitors the chance to learn more about the lives of the enslaved workers who put Washington's ideas into practice.

Greenhouse and garden

The Top 10 of Everything

The ornate Great Hall
of the Library of Congress

Moments in History   42
US Presidents   44
Places of African
    American History   46
Historic Homes and Buildings   48
Memorials and Monuments   50
Museums   54
Art Galleries   56
Green Spaces   58
Outdoor Activities   60
Off the Beaten Path   62
Children's Attractions   64
Theaters   66
Restaurants   68
Washington, DC for Free   70
Festivals and
    Cultural Events   72
Trips from Washington, DC   74

TOP10 Moments in History

Armies at the end of the Civil War on Pennsylvania Avenue in Washington, DC

1 Foundation of the Federal City

The US Constitution, ratified in 1788, provided and planned for "a District (not exceeding ten Miles square) as may, by Cession of Particular States..., become the Seat of the Government of the United States."

2 Layout and Design

In 1790, George Washington selected Pierre Charles L'Enfant, a French engineer, to lay out the city. The plan was influenced by Versailles and the city of Paris.

3 Expansion

Thomas Jefferson began western expansion by organizing the Lewis and Clark expedition in 1803. The C&O Canal, built between 1828 and 1850, and the Baltimore and Ohio Railroad, founded in 1828, provided a means of commerce through the mountains and launched a period of prosperity. New states were added to the Union, and bitter divisions arose connected to the issue of slavery.

4 War of 1812

The United States declared war on Britain in 1812, seeking freedom of marine trade and the security of US seamen. In 1814, British troops entered the capital and burned government buildings, including the White House and the Capitol. If it had not rained, the whole city might have burned down.

5 Civil War

Conflict between the Union and the seceding Southern states began on April 12, 1861, plunging Washington and the nation into crisis. Union supporters, joined by thousands of Black people escaping slavery in the South, doubled the city's population in four years. Although threatened, the city was never taken by Confederate troops and, when the war ended in 1865, Washington was unharmed.

The burning of the city in 1812

6 McMillan Plan
The McMillan Plan of 1901, so named for its congressional supporter, Senator James McMillan, was the first ever application of city planning in the US. It created much of the layout of the Mall and President's Park.

7 New Deal
The Roosevelt era (1933–45) brought tremendous growth to the city. Efforts to bring the nation out of the Great Depression increased the size and number of government agencies, and provided direct funds for construction. Most of the buildings in the Federal Triangle, the completion of the Supreme Court, and the National Gallery of Art were New Deal works.

8 World War II
More than 10 percent of the US population of approximately 115 million was in uniform at the peak of the war, and the central management of all of these troops remained in Washington, DC.

Dr. Martin Luther King, Jr.

9 March on Washington
African American leaders led 250,000 people to rally before the Lincoln Memorial on August 28, 1963 in support of equal rights. Dr. Martin Luther King, Jr.'s eloquent dream for America gave impetus to the struggle.

10 Statehood
DC is the only part of the US without representation in Congress. A statehood bill was passed in 2020, but has been stalled in the Senate for now. It is slated to be called the "State of Washington, Douglass Commonwealth" to honor Frederick Douglass (see p47), the famous abolitionist.

TOP 10 AMENDMENTS OF THE CONSTITUTION

United States Constitution

1 Inherent Rights
Freedom of religion, speech, the press, assembly, and seeking redress of citizen grievances.

2 Legality of Arms
The right of the people to keep and bear arms.

3 Quartering of Soldiers
Freedom from housing soldiers in private homes in peacetime and in war, except as prescribed by law.

4 Unjustified Searches
Freedom from unreasonable search and seizure of people, houses, and effects without a warrant.

5 Limits on Prosecutors
A grand jury indictment is required before trial; a person cannot be tried more than once for the same crime; a person cannot be forced to testify against himself; a person's property cannot be confiscated without compensation.

6 Protection of the Accused
Accused persons will be given a trial by a jury of peers, be informed of the charges, be able to confront witnesses, and be represented by counsel.

7 Civil Case Jury Trial
In common law, parties have a right to a trial by jury.

8 Unjust Punishment
The government cannot require excessive bail, impose excessive fines, or use cruel or unusual punishment.

9 Limited Scope
The stated rights do not limit other rights.

10 State Powers
All powers not granted to the US government belong to the states.

TOP 10 US Presidents

George Washington

is little doubt that the Federalist Papers, which he co-authored, helped gain its ratification.

5 Andrew Jackson
After Jackson's success (1829–37) as a leader in the Battle of New Orleans in 1814–15, he was regarded as a national hero. His popularity helped him win battles with Congress and with private business interests over issues such as banking and tariffs.

6 Abraham Lincoln
Often referred to as one of the greatest ever political leaders in any nation, Lincoln (1861–5) overcame inexpressible odds in preserving the Union and beginning the process of freeing those who were enslaved.

1 George Washington
The first president of the United States, Washington (1789–97), was never greater than when he refused to interpret the position of president as equivalent to "king."

2 John Adams
Adams (1797–1801) was among the young nation's most experienced diplomats, having managed affairs in Europe. He was the first US vice president, under Washington.

7 Theodore Roosevelt
The dawning of the 20th century brought an energetic and activist president to the helm. Roosevelt (1901–9) became famous for his military exploits in the Spanish–American War, but is best known for his opposition to business monopolies and pursuing a strong foreign policy. He also established the National Parks system in the US.

3 Thomas Jefferson
Jefferson (1801–9) is remembered for his embrace of democracy and his strong opposition to federal power.

John Adams

8 Franklin D. Roosevelt
Roosevelt's (1933–45) efforts to overcome the Great Depression never succeeded in the broadest sense, but they inculcated the federal government with a sense of respect for the rights and needs of the common person and the poorest of the poor. He led valiantly during World War II.

4 James Madison
Madison (1809–17) demurred when he was called "the Father of the Constitution," stating that many minds had contributed, but there

⑨ John F. Kennedy

Kennedy (1961–3) brought an unprecedented style and flair to the presidency and can be credited with possibly the most important action of the 20th century – the prevention of nuclear war over Soviet missiles placed in Cuba. His assassination cut short his pursuit of a plan for progressive social programs, including more freedom and justice for African Americans.

John F. Kennedy

⑩ Barack Obama

A key figure in American politics, Barack Hussein Obama was the first African American to be elected President. He spent two terms (2009-2017) as commander-in-chief and successfully led the country out of the Great Recession. He signed into law healthcare reform, and ended the war in Iraq as well. In 2009 he was awarded the Nobel Peace Prize for his efforts to fortify international diplomacy.

Barack Obama

TOP 10 FIRST LADIES

Hillary Clinton

1 Martha Washington
Martha established the role of the First Lady imitated by her successors. She was famous for accompanying George on military campaigns.

2 Dolley Madison
Dolley's social appeal greatly helped her slightly awkward husband.

3 Sarah Polk
The wife of James K. Polk (1845–9) was a strong force in the administration, writing speeches for the president.

4 Mary Todd Lincoln
Mary supported Lincoln and the Union in the Civil War and worked to promote the emancipation of enslaved people.

5 Eleanor Roosevelt
Eleanor's interests were equal rights and social justice. She greatly increased the diplomatic role of the First Lady.

6 Jacqueline Kennedy
A stylish socialite, Jackie was an instant hit with the public and visiting diplomats.

7 Lady Bird Johnson
Wife of Lyndon B. Johnson (1963–9), Lady Bird's beautification projects had a direct impact on DC.

8 Hillary Clinton
The former First Lady (1993–2001) has gone on to be a Senator (2001–9), Secretary of State (2009–13) and presidential candidate (2016).

9 Michelle Obama
A Harvard Law School graduate, she was a top lawyer, Chicago city administrator, and community outreach worker before becoming the 44th First Lady (2009–2017).

10 Jill Biden
A doctor of Education and a college professor, Jill Biden served as second lady from 2009 to 2017, before becoming the 46th First Lady in 2021.

Places of African American History

1 Lincoln Memorial
This memorial *(see p86)* touches the hearts of all African Americans because of Abraham Lincoln's steadfastness in ending slavery in the US. It was here that Martin Luther King, Jr. made his "I Have a Dream" speech.

Martin Luther King, Jr. Memorial

2 Martin Luther King, Jr. Memorial
MAP N5 ▪ 1964 Independence Ave, SW ▪ Open 24 hours daily

The Mall's first monument to an African American, the Martin Luther King, Jr. memorial commemorates the work of the Baptist minister, civil rights activist, and inspirational orator. The two massive stone sculptures were designed by the Chinese sculptor Lei Yixin.

3 Metropolitan African Methodist Episcopal Church
MAP P2 ▪ 1518 M St, NW

This church was important in sheltering enslaved people before the Civil War, and its pulpit has hosted many respected speakers, including Frederick Douglass, Martin Luther King, Jr., and Jesse Jackson. The funeral of civil-rights activist Rosa Parks was held here in 2005.

4 Anacostia Community Museum
MAP E4 ▪ 1901 Fort Place, SE ▪ Open 10am–5pm daily

This museum explores the role that African Americans have played in the culture of the nation as well as in contemporary urban communities.

5 Frederick Douglass National Historic Site
Frederick Douglass, a former enslaved person, made many speeches for the rights of African Americans, and was an adviser to Abraham Lincoln. He and his wife, Anna, moved into this Gothic-Italian-style house *(see p49)* in 1877. In the garden is a humble stone hut nicknamed "The Growlery," which Douglass used as a study.

6 Mary McLeod Bethune Council House
After picking cotton as a child, Bethune rose to be a leading educator of African Americans and an activist for equal rights. Her home *(see p49)* was headquarters of the National Council of Negro Women. She was also an adviser to Franklin D. Roosevelt.

Mary McLeod Bethune Council House

7 Mount Zion United Methodist Church

MAP L2 ■ 1334 29th St, NW ■ 202-234-0148 ■ Services 10:50am Sun ■ Open by appt at other times

Founded in 1816, this was believed to be the first Black congregation in the District. The original building was an important stop on the Underground Railroad. The present red-brick church was built in 1884. A small cottage holds artifacts reflecting the Black history of Georgetown.

8 Lincoln Park

Lincoln Park statue

This park does justice to its dedication to Lincoln. The 1974 Robert Berks statue of Mary McLeod Bethune (see p82) shows the great educator passing the tools of culture on to younger generations. The Emancipation Statue (see p82) by Thomas Ball (1876) shows Lincoln holding his Proclamation in the presence of an enslaved person escaping chains.

9 African American Civil War Memorial and Museum

MAP Q1 ■ 1925 Vermont Ave, NW ■ 202-667-2667 ■ Open 11am–4pm Mon–Sat by appt ■ www.afroamcivilwar.org

This small museum uses artifacts, photographs, and exhibits to highlight the contributions of the more than 200,000 African Americans who fought in the Civil War.

10 National Museum of African American History and Culture

The impressive collection of artifacts and memorabilia at this museum (see pp32–3) document the history of African Americans, along with their contributions to areas such as music, sports, and the visual arts.

TOP 10 AFRICAN AMERICAN FIGURES IN DC'S HISTORY

Activist Mary Church Terrell

1 Ralph Bunche
The first African American to receive the Nobel Peace Prize, because of his diplomatic efforts in the UN.

2 Duke Ellington
The musical genius was a native of Washington. He played his first paid performance on U Street.

3 Frederick Douglass
Celebrated 19th-century abolitionist and Black statesman (see p43).

4 Paul Lawrence Dunbar
Dunbar rose from poverty to gain recognition as a poet – the first African American to do so – publishing his first collection in 1892.

5 Harriet Tubman
The best-known figure who freed those enslaved via the secret Underground Railroad network in the 19th century.

6 Mary McLeod Bethune
This pioneering educator and civil rights leader established the National Council of Negro Women in DC in 1935 (see p51).

7 Mary Church Terrell
One of the first African American women to earn a degree, this civil rights activist led protests that helped to end segregation in DC.

8 Eleanor Holmes Norton
Norton has been effective as a non-voting House member, lobbying to promote Washington issues.

9 Walter E. Washington
Mayor of Washington from 1975 to 1979, the first elected mayor in the city for over 100 years.

10 Alma Thomas
A seminal abstract artist and teacher, Thomas was Howard University's first Fine Arts Department graduate.

🔟 Historic Homes and Buildings

1 Carnegie Library
MAP Q3 ▪ 801 K St, NW

Philanthropist Andrew Carnegie campaigned to build libraries across America and funded 1,679 in all. This magnificent Beaux Arts building has been restored and is occupied by the Historical Society of Washington, DC.

2 Decatur House
Stephen Decatur, a renowned naval hero, built this Federal-style townhouse (see p102) in 1818. It now houses the White House Historical Association, but has been preserved to evoke 19th-century middle-class America. The Carriage House next door was once a service wing that housed enslaved workers in the 1820s and 1830s.

3 Gadsby's Tavern Museum
MAP D5 ▪ 134 N Royal St, Alexandria, VA ▪ 703-746-4242 ▪ Open Apr–Oct: 10am–5pm Tue–Sat, 1–5pm Sun–Mon; Nov–Mar: 11am–4pm Wed–Sat, 1–4pm Sun ▪ Adm

Two buildings occupy this site: the 1792 City Hotel, and the 1785 tavern where early American leaders, in-cluding Washington and Jefferson, dined. Today this National Historic Landmark houses a city museum and a fine-dining restaurant.

The facade of Ford's Theatre

4 Ford's Theatre
The theater where Lincoln was shot in 1865 by John Wilkes Booth has been restored by the federal government. It is now a memorial (see p95) to the music- and theater-loving president. There is a museum on site and the building also hosts theater productions.

5 Woodrow Wilson House
MAP M1 ▪ 2340 S St, NW ▪ 202-387-4062 ▪ Open 10am–4pm Wed–Sat, noon–4pm Tue & Sun ▪ Adm

President Woodrow Wilson moved into this Georgian Revival house in 1921 after serving as the 28th presi-dent of the United States. The marble entry, staircase, and solarium are highlights and the Wilson furnishings are from 1924.

The lavish drawing room of Woodrow Wilson House

6 Frederick Douglass National Historic Site

MAP E4 ▪ 1411 W St, SE ▪ 202-426-5961 ▪ Open Apr–Oct: 9am–5pm daily (to 4:30pm Nov–Mar); closed Thanksgiving, Dec 25, Jan 1 ▪ www.nps.gov/frdo

Frederick Douglass and his wife Anna were the very first African American family in Anacostia when they moved to this house (see p46) in 1877. Born into slavery, Douglass became America's most effective anti-slavery speaker and writer.

7 Mary McLeod Bethune Council House

MAP P2 ▪ 1318 Vermont Ave, NW ▪ 202-673-2402 ▪ Open 9am–5pm Thu–Sat ▪ www.nps.gov/mamc

A renowned teacher and activist, Mary Bethune (see p46) bought this Victorian townhouse – now a National Historic Site – in 1935. It is still furnished with her possessions.

The stately Dumbarton Oaks

8 Dumbarton Oaks

This remarkable Federal-style home (1801) is filled with a Harvard-curated collection of Byzantine and pre-Columbian art. The house (see p105) is surrounded by lovely gardens, with an orangery whose walls are draped in a 150-year-old ficus.

9 Old Stone House

The oldest surviving structure in DC (see p107), this evocative building holds demonstrations of crafts and skills of pre-Revolutionary life.

10 Belmont-Paul House

Built in 1800, this enchanting home (see p81) is one of the oldest on Capitol Hill. It is now a museum of women's equality.

TOP 10 ARCHITECTURAL SIGHTS

National Building Museum

1 National Building Museum
Displays examine architecture, design, engineering, and city planning (see p95).

2 Eisenhower Executive Office Building
MAP N4 ▪ 1650 Pennsylvania Ave, NW
The extravagant decoration is a favorite with architecture buffs.

3 Treasury Building
This 1836 Greek Revival building (see p100) retains original features.

4 The Octagon Museum
This building (see p100) is now a museum of architecture and design.

5 Library of Congress
This extensive library (see p79) contains more than 38 million books.

6 Old Post Office Tower
MAP P4 ▪ 1100 Pennsylvania Ave, NW ▪ www.nps.gov/opot
This iconic Romanesque revival building was completed in 1899.

7 Pope-Leighey House
9000 Richmond Hwy, Alexandria, VA ▪ Open 11am–4pm Fri–Mon ▪ Adm ▪ www.woodlawnpopeleighey.org
The city's most innovative Frank Lloyd Wright design.

8 Supreme Court Building
This marble edifice (see p80) never fails to delight.

9 Anderson House
MAP M2 ▪ 2118 Massachusetts Ave, NW ▪ Open 10am–4pm Tue–Sat, noon–4pm Sun
This Beaux Arts mansion was built in 1905 for Ambassador Larz Anderson.

10 Cox's Row
MAP K2 ▪ 3327–29 N St, NW
These Federal-style townhouses in Georgetown are good early 19th-century examples of domestic architecture.

TOP 10 Memorials and Monuments

The Franklin D. Roosevelt Memorial depicting the president and his dog

1 Lincoln Memorial

The majestic monument *(see p86)* to the president who preserved America's unity and began the process of ending slavery is built in the form of a Greek temple. Daniel Chester French designed the enormous statue of a seated Abraham Lincoln in 1915, and it is among America's most inspiring sites, especially for its association with the African American struggle for equality and opportunity.

2 Washington Monument

This spire *(see p87)* is a dominant feature on the city's skyline, 555-ft- (170-m-) high and clad in gleaming white marble. One of the tallest freestanding masonry constructions in the world, built between 1848 and 1884, the obelisk can be seen for miles.

Washington Monument

3 Franklin D. Roosevelt Memorial

This popular memorial *(see p88)*, dedicated by President Clinton in 1997, has four outdoor "rooms," representing Roosevelt's four terms as president. Each is a composition of statues, water, plantings, and engraved quotations. He is accompanied here, as in life, by his beloved Scottish terrier Fala, who rarely left his side. The memorial is a focal point for disability rights activists – Roosevelt was partially paralyzed by polio.

4 Jefferson Memorial

One of Jefferson's favorite Classical designs, the Pantheon in Rome, inspired this graceful monument *(see p88)*. Dedicated in 1943 on the 200th anniversary of his birth, it houses a 19-ft (6-m) bronze statue of him by Rudolph Evans. The temple is especially enchanting when floodlit at night.

5 Vietnam Veterans Memorial

This simple V-shaped black granite wall *(see p86)* features the names of all those who died in this divisive war. The 1982 memorial is the work of Maya Lin, at the time a 21-year-old architecture student at Yale.

⑥ Korean War Veterans Memorial

Nineteen steel statues dominate in this memorial *(see p88)* to the Americans who died in the UN's "police action" in Korea. A wall is etched with faces of actual soldiers. A circular pool invites quiet reflection.

⑦ The Pentagon

MAP C4 ▪ 2024 Pentagon Pedestrian Tunnel, Arlington, VA ▪ defense.gov/Pentagon-Tours

With well over 17 miles (27 km) of corridors, the US military headquarters is the world's largest office. The 60-minute free tour covers 1.5 miles (2.5 km) of the complex and includes military history, the 9/11 Memorial, and the Hall of Heroes. Visitors need to book 14 days in advance.

⑧ World War II Memorial

This memorial *(see p88)* honors the 16 million who served in the US military during World War II, as well as the civilians who helped.

⑨ African American Civil War Memorial

MAP P1 ▪ 1000 U St, NW

"The Spirit of Freedom," a 1996 sculpture by Ed Hamilton, depicts African American Union soldiers facing the opposition.

⑩ Iwo Jima Statue (Marine Corps Memorial)

MAP K5 ▪ 1400 N Meade St, Arlington, VA

Marines struggling to erect the Stars and Stripes on a ridge at Iwo Jima serves as a memorial to all marines who have fought for their country. The Pacific island saw fierce fighting, resulting in 7,000 American deaths, during World War II.

Iwo Jima Statue

TOP 10 STATUES

Abraham Lincoln Memorial

1 Abraham Lincoln
The marble vision *(see p86)* of the president dominates the memorial.

2 Neptune Fountain
Roland Hinton Perry created this grouping at the Library of Congress *(see p79)*.

3 Albert Einstein
MAP M4 ▪ 2101 Constitution Ave, NW
This 1979 bronze by Robert Berks *(see p102)* shows the great thinker in front of the National Academy of Sciences.

4 Benjamin Franklin
MAP P4 ▪ 1100 Pennsylvania Ave, NW
Jacques Jouvenal's statue at the Old Post Office honors Franklin's creation of the US Postal Service.

5 First Division Monument
MAP N4 ▪ State Place & 17th St, NW
A shining tribute to the First Infantry Division of World War I.

6 Stone of Hope
MAP N5 ▪ Martin Luther King Jr. Memorial
Chinese sculptor Lei Yixin created Martin Luther King, Jr.'s statue at the memorial *(see p46)*.

7 Mary McLeod Bethune Memorial
MAP E4 ▪ Lincoln Park
A bronze statue of the educator, civil rights leader, and activist *(see p82)*.

8 Ulysses S. Grant Memorial
This grouping *(see p82)* took Henry Merwin Shrady 20 years to complete.

9 Bust of Sojourner Truth
MAP R5 ▪ Capitol Visitor Center, 1st St, NE
The US Capitol *(see pp12–13)* has a bronze bust of the famous abolitionist.

10 Vietnam Women's Memorial
MAP M5 ▪ National Mall
A statue dedicated to all the nurses and women who served in the Vietnam War.

☆REVOLUTIONARY·WAR·1775–1783☆ FREN

VAL·WAR·1798-1801 ☆ TRIPOLI·1801-1805 ☆ WAR·OF·1812-1815 ☆ FLORIDA·INDIAN·WARS·1835-18

TOP 10 Museums

A Douglas DC-3 aircraft on display at the National Air and Space Museum

1 National Air and Space Museum

The 20th century's love affair with flight, from its intrepid beginnings to the mastery of space travel, is explored here *(see pp20–21)*.

2 National Museum of the American Indian

The Smithsonian's huge collection of material and artifacts related to American Indian art, history, culture, and language moved into its first permanent home in 2004 *(see p85)*.

Exhibits at the National Museum of the American Indian

3 National Museum of Natural History

Must-see exhibits abound: the Hall of Human Origins depicting human evolution over six million years; the FossiLab; the Don Pedro aquamarine and Hope diamond in the National Gem collection; and a stunning mammal exhibit *(see pp28–9)*.

4 National Museum of American History

Combining the "America's Attic" approach with fine contemporary interpretive exhibits, the museum *(see pp22–3)* offers visitors a fascinating look into America's past.

5 United States Holocaust Memorial Museum

Designed by James Ingo Freed and referencing Holocaust sites via its abstract architectural forms, this museum *(see pp86–7)* traces the Holocaust in Europe, grimly detailing the surveillance and the loss of individual rights faced by Jews, political objectors, Romani, the LGBTQ+ community, and disabled people. Moving eyewitness accounts, photographs, and artifacts all help to tell the story.

Previous pages Iwo Jima Statue (Marine Corps Memorial) at sunset

6 National Postal Museum

Mail and fun don't naturally go together, but at this wonderfully conceived museum *(see p81)*, they do. The little Pony Express saddlebags, tunnel-like construction representing the desolate roads faced by the earliest mail carriers, and the mail-sorting railroad car all entertain and inform visitors.

7 International Spy Museum

This fascinating museum *(see p88)* explores the role that spies have played in events throughout history. The exhibitions display equipment, tell the stories of individuals, and reveal their missions and techniques.

8 National Archives of the United States

The Rotunda of the National Archives *(see p88)* displays the foundation documents of America: the Constitution of the United States, the Declaration of Independence, and the Bill of Rights. There are exciting interactive activities in the Public Vaults.

9 National Law Enforcement Museum

MAP Q4 ▪ 444 E St, NW ▪ Open 10am–5pm Fri–Sun ▪ Closed Thanksgiving & Dec 25 ▪ Adm ▪ www.lawenforcementmuseum.org

Known to be the first national museum dedicated to American law enforcement, this remarkable venue has more than 20,000 artifacts on display, which include the U.S. Park Police helicopter, J. Edgar Hoover's desk as well as Al Capone's vest.

National Museum of African American History and Culture

10 National Museum of African American History and Culture

Opened in 2016, this excellent museum *(see pp32–3)* is set in a striking bronze-clad contemporary building on the National Mall. It contains over 35,000 artifacts, including an early 1800's slave cabin, a shawl given to 19th-century abolitionist Harriet Tubman by Queen Victoria, and Chuck Berry's red Cadillac. Due to the museum's popularity, passes are required for timed entry only.

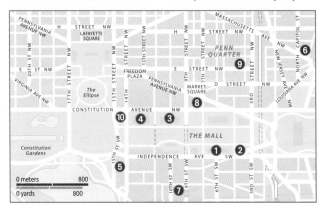

🔟 Art Galleries

Degas' *Dancers at the Barre*

① The Phillips Collection

MAP M2 ■ 1600 21st St, NW ■ 202-387-2151 ■ Open 11am–6pm Tue–Sun ■ Adm ■ www.phillips collection.org

Established in 1921, the Phillips Collection is America's first museum of modern art. It is celebrated for its Impressionist works, including Renoir's *Luncheon of the Boating Party*, Pierre Bonnard's *Open Window*, and Degas' *Dancers at the Barre*.

② National Gallery of Art

Displaying one of the most distinguished art collections in the world, National Gallery of Art *(see pp24–7)* gives its visitors a broad but in-depth look at the development of American and European art from the Middle Ages to the 20th century.

③ National Portrait Gallery

Portraits of remarkable Americans who shaped the country are on display at this gallery *(see p96)*. Its highlights include a complete collection of portraits of all the presidents of America, and American Origins, a chronologically arranged exhibit showcasing encounters between American Indians and European explorers from the early years into the early 20th century.

④ Renwick Gallery

This gallery *(see p99)* is considered by many Washingtonians as their favorite, not least because it is housed in a gorgeous French Renaissance-style building, as well as staging well-organized shows of American crafts. The Grand Salon, previously styled as a 19th-century picture gallery, was the subject of an international design competition to "re-envision" it as a contemporary exhibition space.

⑤ Hirshhorn Museum and Sculpture Garden

The Hirshhorn *(see p85)* exhibits the most varied modern and contemporary art in Washington, DC. The collection of 12,000 artworks by leading artists, from the late 19th century to the present, includes paintings, sculptures, and mixed media, as well as photographs, works on paper, and new media. Exhibitions change frequently, displaying art by emerging or well-known artists, illustrating a major trend, or highlighting historical developments.

An exquisite collection of sculptures at the National Gallery of Art

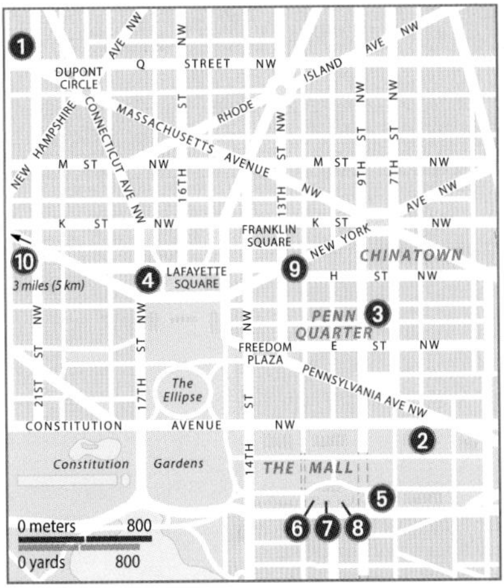

6 Freer Gallery of Art

MAP P5 ■ Jefferson Drive at 12th St, SW ■ 202-633-1000 ■ Open 10am–5:30pm daily ■ www.asia.si.edu

Following extensive renovations, the intimate and tranquil Freer Gallery reopened in 2017, and with the neighboring Sackler Gallery, it now forms the National Museum of Asian Art. The elegant exhibit spaces, with Terrazzo floors, have returned to their original 1923 splendor. Its collection spans 6,000 years with more than 22,000 works. The permanent exhibitions feature art from the Middle East, East Asia, and the Indian subcontinent, while the temporary exhibitions highlight the many cultures represented here.

7 Arthur M. Sackler Gallery

MAP Q5 ■ 1050 Independence Ave, SW ■ 202-633-1000 ■ Open 10am–5:30pm daily; closed Dec 25 ■ www.asia.si.edu

Forming the National Museum of Asian Art, along with the Freer Gallery, the Sackler is a leading center for the study and display of ancient and contemporary Asian art. Its events bring Asian art and philosophies to life, and its occasional presentations of monks carrying out the ritual of sand-painting a mandala are always huge hits.

Bronze Shiva, Arthur M. Sackler Gallery

8 National Museum of African Art

This harmonious building (see p88) brings architectural features common in Africa to one of the Smithsonian's most innovative museums, built principally underground. The wonderful permanent collection provides the best introduction to the role of art in African culture that one could hope to find. The pieces on display include ceramics, musical instruments, textiles, tools, masks, and figurines.

9 National Museum of Women in the Arts

This is the only museum (see p96) in the world dedicated exclusively to displaying the work of women artists, from the Renaissance to the present day. Fascinating and provocative exhibitions explore the work and social role of female artists over the centuries, as well as that of women in general.

10 Kreeger Museum

MAP G5 ■ 2401 Foxhall Rd, NW ■ 202-337-3050 ■ Open 10am–4pm Tue–Sat ■ Tours 10:30am & 1:30pm Tue–Fri, 10:30am, noon, & 2pm Sat ■ Adm ■ www.kreegermuseum.org

This relatively unknown private museum houses Impressionist works by 19th- and 20th-century painters and sculptors such as Rodin, Kandinsky, and Monet, works by Washington artists, and traditional works of art from Africa and Asia.

TOP 10 Green Spaces

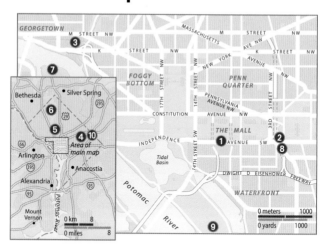

1 Enid A. Haupt Garden

MAP P5 ■ 10th St & Independence Ave, NW ■ Open dawn–dusk daily ■ Tours: mid-May–late Sep: 10am, except federal holidays

These gardens sit on top of the Smithsonian Museums. The Moongate Garden beside the Sackler Gallery reflects the Asian world, with its circular pool, pink granite, and cherry and beech trees. The Fountain Garden, alongside the Museum of African Art, evokes a Moorish ambience, with cascading waters and shaded seats.

2 US Botanic Garden

The glass-walled conservatory building is home to this "living plant

The glass-walled US Botanic Garden

museum" (see p80). Microclimates, such as desert, tropics, and Mediterranean, reveal the variety and beauty of plant adaptations. Outside is the variegated National Garden with an environmental learning center.

3 Chesapeake and Ohio Canal

Boats on this 19th-century 184-mile-(295-km-) waterway (see p105) carried cargo between Maryland and Georgetown for 100 years before the railroad put it out of business. It is now a National Historical Park, a haven for walkers and cyclists. Interpreted canal boat tours depart from the Great Falls Tavern Visitor Center.

4 National Arboretum

MAP E3 ■ 3501 New York Ave, NE ■ 202-245-4523 ■ Open 8am–5pm daily; closed Dec 25 ■ www.usna.usda.gov

An acclaimed bonsai display (see p71), some trees are almost 400 years old, is one of the many collections that flourish on these 446 acres (180 ha). Azaleas, dogwoods, magnolias, boxwoods, and roses abound. A stand of columns, formerly on the US Capitol, adds a classical air.

Cherry trees at Dumbarton Oaks

5 Dumbarton Oaks

Magnificent trees, including ancient oaks, soar above the park and gardens surrounding this historic Federal-style house (see p105). Designed by Beatrix Jones Farrand, the gardens range from formal to more casual settings. In spring, they are a mass of cherry blossom, and from March to October they are ablaze with wisteria, roses, lilies, and perennial borders. Pools and fountains tie the ensemble together.

6 Rock Creek Park
MAP J1 ▪ 5200 Glover Rd, NW ▪ Open dawn–dusk daily, check website for details ▪ www.nps.gov/rocr

This vast National Park meanders with its namesake creek, offering something for everyone: there are lovely woodland trails and nature programs, bicycle paths, tennis courts, a golf course, playing fields, and picnic areas.

7 Theodore Roosevelt Island
MAP L4 ▪ George Washington Memorial Parkway ▪ Open 6am–10pm daily

This wooded island on the Potomac River is the perfect memorial to the president who valued conservation. A 17-ft- (5-m-) statue of Roosevelt is the center-piece of what is otherwise a monument to nature – an unspoiled, idyllic space for birdwatching, hiking, fishing, and relaxing.

Theodore Roosevelt statue

8 Bartholdi Park and Fountain

The French sculptor of the Statue of Liberty, Frédéric Auguste Bartholdi (1834–1904), also created this reflection of *belle époque* majesty. The 30-ft- (9-m-) sculpture's three caryatids support a circular basin surmounted by three tritons. A small garden surrounds the fountain (see p80) like the setting for a gemstone.

9 East Potomac Park
MAP P6 ▪ 14th St, SW

One of Washington's best-kept secrets, this 300-acre- (120-ha-) peninsula has the Potomac River on one side and the boat-filled Washington Channel on the other. A paved walkway traces the waterfront, offering views to runners, walkers, skaters, and fishermen. There is also a 9- and an 18-hole public golf course. In spring thousands of cherry trees burst into lovely blossoms.

The blossoming East Potomac Park

10 Kenilworth Park and Aquatic Gardens
MAP E3 ▪ Aquatic Gardens: 1550 Anacostia Ave, NE; open 8am–4pm daily; closed Jan 1, Thanksgiving, Dec 25 ▪ Park: Kenilworth & Burroughs Aves; open 8am–dusk daily ▪ www.nps.gov/keaq

The 14-acre- (6-ha-) Aquatic Gardens began as a hobby for Civil War veteran Walter Benjamin Shaw in 1882. He later transformed it into a commercial water garden. Now run by the National Park Service, the gardens are known for its ponds, planted with water lilies and lotuses. Visitors can also find local wildlife here. Adjacent Kenilworth Park offers recreational areas and meadows.

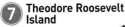

🔟 Outdoor Activities

1 Running
Runners are seen everywhere in Washington. The Mall is a popular spot for running, as are the walkways around the Georgetown Waterfront, the Tidal Basin, East Potomac Park (see p59), the C&O Canal (see p58), and Rock Creek Park (see p59).

2 In-Line Skating
Rock Creek Park (see p59) has been named one of the top 10 sites in the nation for in-line skating, but most bike trails allow skaters as well. Rent skates and protective gear from the numerous in-line skating companies in the area.

3 Boating
Thompson Boat Center: MAP L3; 2900 Virginia Ave, NW; 202-333-9642; open Mar–Oct: hours vary, check website; www.boating indc.com ▪ Washington Sailing Marina: MAP D5; 1 Marina Drive, Dangerfield Island, Alexandria, VA; 703-548-9027; open May–Nov: hours vary, check website; www. boatingindc.com

Georgetown's Thompson Boat Center rents kayaks, rowing shells, canoes, and sailboats to reach Roosevelt Island and tour the waterfront. The Washington Sailing Marina rents sailboats for excursions on the Potomac. Make sure to call in advance about certification requirements.

Cycling by the US Capitol

4 Cycling
Bike and Roll: MAP Q6; 955 L'Enfant Plaza, SW; 202-842-2453; www.bikeandrollldc.com ▪ Capital Bikeshare: www.capitalbikeshare.com

Both the Thompson Boat Center and the Washington Sailing Marina rent bicycles, and Capital Bikeshare has over 500 stations in the area where you may use a credit card to rent a bike for 30 minutes, a day, or three days. Favorite routes are the C&O Canal towpath (see p58) and the Mount Vernon Trail (see pp36–9). Bike and Roll offers tours and rentals.

5 Golf
East Potomac Park: MAP P6; 972 Ohio Drive, SW (Hain's Point); 202-554-7660 ▪ Rock Creek Park Golf Course: MAP D2; 6100 16th St, NW; 202-882-7332 ▪ Langston Golf Course: MAP E3; 2600 Benning Rd, NE; 202-397-8638

There are over 100 golf courses in the vicinity. Public courses include

Sailboats at Washington Harbour

East Potomac Park and the Rock Creek Park Golf Course. Langston Golf Course, a few minutes from Capitol Hill, was among the first African American courses in the US.

6 Informal Team Sports

Volleyball, dodgeball, rugby, softball, kickball, team Frisbee, and even polo are played on various fields at the western end of the Mall.

7 Hiking

www.trails.com

The 4-mile- (7-km-) Western Ridge Trail and 5-mile- (8-km-) Valley Trail, both in Rock Creek Park (see p59), are scenic and gentle. The 11.5-mile- (18.5-km-) Capital Crescent Trail follows the old B&O Railroad route through Georgetown north to Bethesda.

Hikers on snow-clad trails

8 Tennis

East Potomac Park Tennis Center: MAP P6; 1090 Ohio Drive, SW; 202-554-5962; www.eastpotomactennis.com

The East Potomac Park Tennis Center is operated by the National Park Service. Indoor courts are available too.

9 Horseback Riding

Rock Creek Horse Center: MAP J2; 5100 Glover Rd, NW; 202-362-0117; open 10am–6pm Mon–Fri, 9am–5pm Sat & Sun; www.rockcreekhorsecenter.com

The Rock Creek Park Horse Center provides scheduled trail rides and riding lessons for all levels.

10 Ziplining

Go Ape: 6129 Needwood Lake Drive, Derwood, MD; 800-971-8271; www.goape.com

Go Ape offers canopy walks, Tarzan swings, and long ziplines.

TOP 10 SPECTATOR SPORTS

The Washington Football Team

1 Washington Football Team
This National Football League team is a year-round local obsession. Games are at FedEx Field in Maryland. Tickets at www.ticketmaster.com

2 Washington Wizards
The National Basketball Association team plays at the Capital One Arena (see p95). Buy tickets at the box office.

3 Washington Capitals
The National Hockey League team plays its home games at the Capital One Arena.

4 DC United
Audi Field 100 Potomac Ave, SW ▪ 202-587-5467 ▪ www.dcunited.com
Audi Field is home to professional soccer.

5 Baseball
Major league baseball team the Washington Nationals play at Nationals Park in DC, while the Baltimore Orioles play at Camden Yards in Baltimore.

6 Washington Mystics
The women's professional basketball team plays home games at the Entertainment & Sports Arena.

7 Citi Open
www.citiopentennis.com
This mid-summer tournament attracts major tennis pros.

8 Georgetown University Basketball
3700 O St, NW ▪ 202-397-SEAT
The Hoyas provide fast-paced action at the Capital One Arena.

9 University of Maryland Athletics
College Park, MD ▪ www.umterps.com
ACC football and national basketball teams lead a varied program.

10 Naval Academy Football
The spectacle of these games is unmatched. Schedule and tickets: www.navysports.com

Off the Beaten Path

Statue of George Mason

1 George Mason Memorial

MAP N6 ■ www.nps.gov/gemm

Sometimes called the "forgotten Founding Father," George Mason was instrumental in framing the US Constitution and creating the Bill of Rights. Located near the Jefferson Memorial, the Mason Memorial is an open plaza with flower gardens and a fountain. A statue of a smiling, seated Mason is popular with visitors, who sit beside him to have their picture taken.

2 Kenilworth Aquatic Gardens

Laid out in 1882, these gardens (see p59) feature numerous ponds filled with lotus and water lilies that bloom from May to July. A trail through the surrounding Anacostia River marshlands makes this a fascinating stop for nature- and bird-lovers.

3 The Old Stone House

This charming blue granite Georgetown house (see p107) dates from 1765, making it the oldest building in the Washington, DC area. In constant use as a shop or home until its purchase by the government in 1953, it offers a fascinating look at what 18th-century life was like. Behind the vernacular house is an inviting Colonial Revival garden.

4 Lockkeeper's House

MAP N4 ■ Corner of 17th St and Constitution Ave, NW ■ Open 1–4pm Mon–Thu, 10am–4pm Fri & Sat

This small stone building offers a unique insight into DC's colorful past. In the 1800s, a branch of the C&O Canal ran where the avenue is today, and it was the keeper's job to operate the locks, raising and lowering passing barges, and to collect toll.

5 National Postal Museum

This museum (see p81) should be high on any visitor's list for the sheer fun it has relating the story of the American postal service. Historic biplanes hang from the high ceiling, while a real stagecoach is frozen in time, rushing mail to the wild west. Other exhibits include rare and unusual stamps, artifacts from the Pony Express, and even mail carried by Amelia Earhart on her famous transatlantic flight.

National Postal Museum

6 National Museum of Health and Medicine

MAP C2 ■ 2500 Linden Lane, Silver Spring, MD 20910 ■ 301-319-3300 ■ Open 10am–5:30pm daily ■ www.medicalmuseum.mil

Established by the US Army in 1862 to collect and study specimens for the advancement of Army medicine and surgery, this unique collection holds over 25 million fascinating (if somewhat morbid and not for everyone) items, including photos, historic medical artifacts, and preserved human remains. Exhibits include Civil War-era bones and skulls showing battle wounds, and the bullet that killed President Abraham Lincoln in 1865.

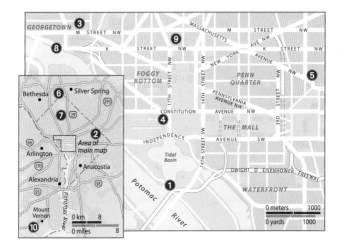

7 Peirce Mill

MAP J3 ■ 2401 Tilden St, NW
■ 202-895-6070 ■ Open Mar: 10am–
4pm Sat & Sun; Apr–Oct: 10am–4pm
Fri–Sun; Nov–Feb: noon–4pm Sat &
Sun ■ www.nps.gov/rocr

This historic grist mill in Rock Creek
Park (see p59) was built in the 1820s
and restored in the early 2000s. A
tour of the mill offers a glimpse into
DC's past, and you can enjoy a hike
or picnic by sparkling Rock Creek.
Demonstrations of the mill grinding
grain are held from April to October,
11am to 2pm every second and
fourth Saturday.

8 Georgetown Waterfront Park

This pretty, tree-shaded park
(see p106) offers fine views of the
busy Potomac from Lincoln Center
to old Georgetown. Benches and
a waterfront walkway make it a
good place for relaxing, strolling,
and picnicking.

9 National Geographic Museum

Anyone who has been thrilled by
National Geographic magazine or TV
documentaries will enjoy this small
museum (see p101) that showcases
the photography of the magazine
as well as constantly changing
exhibits that highlight current stories
and the work of the Society. Oddities
abound, such as the 3D model of the
Grand Canyon on the ceiling.

10 George Washington's Distillery

5513 Mount Vernon Memorial Hwy
Alexandria, VA ■ Open Apr–Oct:
10am–5pm daily ■ Adm ■ www.
mountvernon.org

Washington's most successful
business venture was making whiskey. His distillery and grist mill,
located about 3 miles (5 km) from
the Mount Vernon estate (see pp36–9),
operate using methods and equipment typical of Washington's era.
Entrance to the site is included as
part of the Mount Vernon ticket, but
it can also be purchased separately.

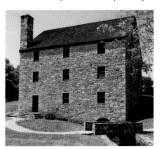

George Washington's Distillery

🔟 Children's Attractions

National Air and Space Museum

1 National Air and Space Museum

Kids will be inspired by the rockets and aircraft, while parents and grandparents reminisce over early days of aviation and space flight *(see pp20–21)*.

2 Six Flags America and Hurricane Harbor

13710 Central Avenue, Upper Marlboro, MD 20721 ■ Open Six Flags: Jun–Aug: 10:30am–6pm (hours vary) daily, Sep–May: days and hours vary; Hurricane Harbor: Jun–Sep: 11am–7pm daily (May: days and hours vary) ■ Adm ■ www.sixflags.com/america

Six Flags features ten roller coasters, along with plenty of rides for smaller kids, who will also adore Looney Tunes Movie Town. Hurricane Harbor area of the site has a huge water park with a dozen water slides and a massive wave pool.

3 National Zoo

The animals in the city's zoo *(see p112)* inhabit spacious, re-created natural habitats. The Speedwell Conservation Carousel showcases endangered species under a colorful open-air pavilion.

4 The Capital Wheel at National Harbor

MAP D6 ■ 116 Waterfront St, MD 20745 ■ Open 10am–10pm daily ■ Adm ■ www.thecapitalwheel.com

The Capital Wheel lifts visitors 180 ft (55 m) above the ground in climate-controlled gondolas, offering fine views up and down the Potomac River. Nearby is "The Awakening", a sculpture of a yawning giant emerging from the earth.

5 Georgetown Waterfront Park

This park *(see p106)* features a huge fountain at the entrance, which is a big hit with kids in the summer. There are spacious grassy parks on either side where you can have a picnic. In winter, the fountain is transformed into DC's largest ice rink.

6 Wolftrap Children's Theatre in the Woods

1551 Trap Rd, Vienna, VA 22182 ■ Open late Jun–mid-Aug, check website for times ■ Adm ■ www. wolftrap.org

This endearing venue offers dance, music, puppetry, and plays for kids age four and up. Programs encourage children to sing, dance, and get on stage with the performers.

Six Flags America roller coaster

Carousel on the Mall

MAP P5 ▪ 900 Jefferson Drive, SW ▪ Open 10am–5pm daily, weather permitting; closed Dec 25 ▪ Adm

In front of the Arts and Industries Building at the Smithsonian, this delightful vintage carousel with brightly painted, hand-carved animals is a bit of old-world fun.

 International Spy Museum

From a spy letter penned by George Washington to James Bond's Aston Martin, this unique museum (see p88) offers a kid-pleasing glimpse into the world of spies and espionage. The museum's thousands of artifacts include gadgets such as a German World War II Enigma machine, an umbrella that fires poison pellets, and a KGB lipstick gun. Kids can learn about spies and spymasters, gadget makers, espionage, and how spying shaped the world. They can also test their code-cracking skills.

 National Museum of American History

This kid-friendly museum (see pp22–3) has some great hands-on action for its younger visitors. Activities including the DraperSpark!Lab with interactive exhibits exploring the process of invention, are targeted at children aged 6 to 12, but the Wegmans Wonderplace and Object Project are also geared towards younger tots.

10 National Museum of Natural History

There is plenty to interest young visitors here (see pp28–9), in particular the FossiLab where staff remove fossils from rock and loose sediment, and repair, conserve, and photograph them. There is also the Dinosaur Hall, which contains a cast of a nest of dinosaur eggs and reconstructions of dinosaur skeletons. Q?rius (pronounced "curious") encourages teens, tweens, and children (and adults) to hold and interact with objects such as crocodile heads and elephant tusks. The Live Butterfly Pavilion is home to exquisite species from around the world.

TOP 10 PLAYGROUNDS

The National Building Museum

1 National Building Museum
Construct a Lego wall, wear a hard hat, and shop at a hardware store (see p95).

2 National Arboretum
An environmental friendly playground (see p58) with a train exhibit.

3 Old Town Alexandria
Ride the King Street Trolley and enjoy the Scavenger Hunt at Old Town (see p111).

4 District Wharf
MAP Q6 ▪ 760 Maine Ave, SW
Play oversized games and roast s'mores at the firepit near the pier.

5 Clemyjontri Park
MAP B3 ▪ 6317 Georgetown Pike, McLean ▪ www.fairfaxcounty.gov
Fun rides and a picnic pavillion fully adapted for children with specific needs.

6 National Museum of the American Indian ImagiNations Activity Center
Take part in hands-on activities such as playing drums and an interactive quiz show (see p85).

7 Discovery Theater
MAP P5 ▪ 1100 Jefferson Drive, SW ▪ www.discoverytheater.org
School-going kids will enjoy puppet shows, music, storytelling, and mimes.

8 National Museum of African American History and Culture
Kids here (see p55) can drive an antique car and dance with Step Afrika!

9 Pentagon Row
MAP K4 ▪ 1101 South Joyce St, Arlington ▪ www.pentagonrow skating.com
A great place for kids to play. In winter it becomes an ice skating rink.

10 Udvar-Hazy Center
Kids can dress as astronauts and get to touch the Space Shuttle here (see p21).

🔟 Theaters

Visitors at the Lincoln Museum in the historic Ford's Theatre

1 Ford's Theatre
The tragedy of Abraham Lincoln's assassination here in 1865 kept this theater *(see p95)* closed for over 100 years, but now it is the home of a vibrant theater company as well as being a museum, center for learning, and historic landmark.

2 Arena Stage
MAP Q6 ■ 1101 6th St, SW
■ 202-554-9066 ■ www.arenastage.org
Internationally renowned as a pioneering non-profit theater for over six decades, Arena has produced plenty of high-quality drama. The Arena reopened at Mead Center for American Theater in late 2010, making it the leading center for production, development, and study of American theater.

3 Folger Theatre
Visitors are treated to a rare experience in this Elizabethan-style theater *(see p79)*, which strongly suggests the setting in which Shakespeare's works were originally performed. Works of the Bard and his near contemporaries are featured, and performances of medieval and baroque music fill the rich, varied schedule.

4 Anacostia Playhouse
MAP D4 ■ 2020 Shannon Pl, SE
■ 202-290-2328 ■ www.anacostia playhouse.com
This small theater began life as the H Street Playhouse, and moved to this location in 2013. It hosts new plays, jazz concerts, community fundraisers, and more.

5 Kennedy Center
With performances ranging from Shakespeare to Sondheim, from gripping drama and opera to light-hearted comedies and musicals, the theater productions at this arts center *(see p99)* are almost always critically acclaimed. There are a variety of performance spaces catering to different styles, seating from just a few hundred people to more than 2,000.

East Terrace at the Kennedy Center

6 Woolly Mammoth Theatre Company
MAP Q4 ▪ 641 D St, NW ▪ 202-393-3939 ▪ www.woollymammoth.net

Widely acknowledged as the city's most daring theater company, Woolly Mammoth stages new, innovative, and thought-provoking productions.

7 National Theatre
MAP P4 ▪ 1321 Pennsylvania Ave, NW ▪ 202-628-6161 ▪ www.thenationaldc.com

Opened in 1835, this wonderful venue hosts top touring shows. A parade of stars and groups such as the Ziegfeld Follies have performed here. Many Broadway classics have staged their premiere here, including *Showboat* and *West Side Story*.

Entrance to the National Theatre

8 GALA Hispanic Theatre
MAP D3 ▪ 3333 14th St, NW ▪ 202-234-7174 ▪ www.galatheatre.org

The recipient of many honors, this award-winning theater mounts performances in Spanish with simultaneous English translation. Brilliant productions of works from the classical to the absurd attract a mixed crowd.

9 Studio Theatre
MAP P2 ▪ 1501 14th St, NW ▪ www.studiotheatre.org

Off-Broadway hits, classics, and experimental fare make up the season at this performance landmark with four theater spaces.

10 Harman Center for the Arts
MAP Q4 ▪ 610 F St, NW

As well as being an expanded stage for the Shakespeare Theatre Company, the Harman Center also offers great theater and ballet performances.

TOP 10 ENTERTAINMENT VENUES

A discussion at Lisner Auditorium

1 Lisner Auditorium
MAP M3 ▪ 730 21st St, NW
This George Washington University theater features world music, classical orchestras, and discussions.

2 Warner Theatre
MAP P4 ▪ 513 13th St, NW
You'll find Broadway shows, comedians, and concerts here.

3 Carter Barron Amphitheatre
MAP D2 ▪ 4850 Colorado Ave, NW
Open-air stage in Rock Creek Park *(see p59)*. It is currently closed for renovation.

4 Coolidge Auditorium
MAP S5 ▪ Library of Congress, 10 1st St, SE
A hall in the Library of Congress *(see p79)* used for classical music performances.

5 Capital One Arena
The home *(see p95)* of DC's basketball and hockey teams has many attractions beyond the games.

6 Nationals Park
MAP E4 ▪ 1500 S Capitol St, SE
Home to the Washington Nationals baseball team, this park is a LEED certified green sports stadium.

7 DAR Constitution Hall
MAP N4 ▪ 1776 D St, NW
The largest concert hall in DC.

8 Lincoln Theatre
MAP P1 ▪ 1215 U St, NW
An intimate setting for an eclectic mix of jazz and popular works of theatre.

9 Wolf Trap National Park for the Performing Arts
1551 & 1635 Trap Rd, Vienna, VA
An open-air venue for all the big names in entertainment.

10 Jiffy Lube Live
7800 Cellar Door Drive, Bristow, VA ▪ Rte I-66 to exit 44
International rock stars perform at this open-air arena.

🔟 Restaurants

1 Central Michel Richard

The late Michel Richard was a Brittany born chef who rose to fame by adding a French twist on modern American cuisine. His namesake bistro *(see p91)* close to the Capitol serves sizeable plates of delicious comfort food, such as braised lamb shanks with spaetzle, small egg, and flour dough dumplings.

Chic interiors of the Blue Duck Tavern

2 Blue Duck Tavern

Capturing the region's culinary traditions, Blue Duck Tavern *(see p103)* serves American fare in a contemporary rustic ambience. While it boasts a Michelin star, it keeps things low-key. The menu includes fresh and simple food from the Mid-Atlantic region, prepared using time-honoured cooking methods, along with modern technology. The Obamas celebrated their 17th wedding anniversary here.

3 Westend Bistro

Located in the Ritz-Carlton, this posh restaurant *(see p103)* adds European accents to fine American ingredients. On offer is a hyper-personalized Chef's Table experience which includes a three-hour-long meal of five courses that must be arranged for 48 hours in advance. The bistro's sophisticated and cozy decor is credited to the award-winning DC architects Adamstein & Demetrou.

4 Vermilion

Seasonal, simple and modern restaurant offering American fare, Vermilion *(see p115)* pairs the changing tasting menu with an extensive list of Virginia wines. Notable dishes from the farm-to-table menu include spicy steak tartare and day boat scallops with beets, stone fruit, and oxtail. For dessert try the creatively flavored ice creams such as sweet corn and burnt honey. The top floor seats are great for people watching.

5 Obelisk

Small and cozy, Obelisk *(see p103)* offers a fixed-price menu of the finest Italian dishes that change daily. The antipasti assortment of small plates consistently stars creamy Burrata. Pasta is shortly followed by meat or fish, and dinner is concluded with cheese and a dessert course. Wine pairings at additional charge.

6 Old Ebbitt Grill

Innkeeper William E. Ebbitt's plush, old-school restaurant *(see p97)* is housed in a Beaux-Arts building that was once the old B. F. Keith's Theater. The restaurant is popular for its oyster menu, and also serves hearty dishes such as shrimp spaghettini, steak frites, and burgers.

7 Marcel's

Enjoy classic French-Belgian fare at Marcel's *(see p103)*, which is known to be one of Washington DC's most highly-rated gourmet restaurants. Risen from the ranks of dishwasher to Michelin-starred chef, Robert Wiedmaier deserves the many accolades he has received since the opening of this sumptuous restaurant in 1999. Diners can choose one of four *prix-fixe* dinners ranging from four to seven courses, and can opt for caviar service. Private dining is also available for upto 120 guests.

8 Rasika

In Sanskrit Rasika means "flavors". This award-winning and popular Indian restaurant *(see p97)*, owned by acclaimed restaurateur Ashok Baja, brings modern and innovative Indian fine dining to Washington, DC. Dishes include flavorful curries and tandoori (clay oven baked) food. Be sure to give the *palak chaat* (crispy baby spinach with sweet yogurt and chutney) a try.

Chefs at work, Iron Gate

9 Iron Gate

À la carte, or family-style Mediterranean fare is served here *(see p103)*. Try the multi-course tasting menu set by chef Anthony Chittum and his talented team. Enjoy al fresco dining on the wisteria-strewn garden patio. The dining room features dishes centered on a wood-burning hearth and rotisserie. Advance reservations are recomended.

10 1789

This eclectic and historic Federal-style townhouse *(see p109)* serves a medley of lamb, oysters, and other dishes. You can also opt for the tasting menu of four, five or six courses. The six elegant dining rooms are beautifully decorated with American antiques, historical equestrian prints, and Limoges china. The Bar & Club Room adjacent to the restaurant has a laid-back vibe. It boasts a large mahogany bar and chic leather seating.

Dining room of the award-winning restaurant, Rasika

🔟 Washington, DC for Free

Visitors exploring paintings inside the US Capitol

① Animal Magic

One of the best free places to spend a day outdoors is the National Zoo *(see p112)*. There are all the usual animals but one of the biggest draws is the giant pandas: Mei Xiang, Tian Tian, and the young cub, Xiao Qi Ji.

② Architectural Gems

Washington DC's superlative architecture is all around you, but is typified by three very remarkable buildings: the National Archives *(see p88)*; the Library of Congress Jefferson Building *(see p79)*, and Union Station *(see p79)*. You can see the first two on a free guided tour; Union Station is open to all.

Union Station splendor

③ Capitol Walking Tour

One of the best freebies in town is the walking tour of the US Capitol building *(see pp12–13)*. It melds art and architecture, every element of which celebrates the vision of America's Founding Fathers.

④ Children's Theater

The National Theatre *(see p67)* offers free kid-oriented Saturday morning entertainment at 9:30am and 11am – tickets are issued 30 minutes beforehand. Shows range from short plays such as Snow White and the Seven Dwarves to magic, puppetry, and music of all sorts.

⑤ Live! Concert Series on the Plaza

MAP P4 ■ www.rrbitc.com

From July to August, some of DC's best free music can be found in the Woodrow Wilson Plaza at the Ronald Reagan Building. Top entertainers perform Monday to Friday. Pack a picnic, or visit the adjacent food court.

⑥ Millennium Stage Summer Series

The Kennedy Center *(see p99)* offers a free performance on the Millennium Stage every day through the summer. Offerings include music, dance, poetry, comedy, and theater.

7 Free Flicks

MAP P5 ▪ www.metrobardc.com

During the summer, metrobar plays movies on a giant outdoor screen and offers free weekly movie nights (usually on Thursdays). Other outdoor cinema sites include Adams Morgan and Georgetown Waterfront Park (see p106). Bring a blanket and snacks (no alcohol) and enjoy the show.

8 Green Escape

The US Botanical Garden (see p80) offers a lush, free refuge to Mall-weary visitors. The vast and beautiful conservatory shelters over 4,000 varieties of plants from around the world. Favorite exhibits include the Jungle, the Orchid Collection, and the Children's Garden.

9 Priceless Plantings

At the 640-acre- (260-ha-) National Arboretum, walkers and cyclists (see p58) are free to explore the myriad paths leading to such delights as a hidden pagoda in the Japanese Stroll Garden. From mid-April to May, tens of thousands of azaleas are in bloom.

The verdant National Arboretum

10 Stroll Southwest Waterfront

MAP D4 ▪ Water St, SW

Lined with picturesque houseboats, yatchs, and sailboats, this is a wonderful place for a leisurely stroll on the waterfront. The diversity of Washington is on parade here, with live performances, unique stores, as well as many restaurants to choose from – ranging from casual dining to upscale seafood.

TOP 10 BUDGET TIPS

Washington, DC Metrorail station

1 The Metrorail is fast, efficient, and affordable. Fares are higher during rush hour (morning and afternoon), so try to time travels for the middle of the day and the evening.

2 Free Tours by Foot offers walking tours in various DC locations. They are not exactly free though – at the end of the tour you are asked to make a donation. See www.freetoursbyfoot.com/washington-dc-tours for all details.

3 DC street vendors can be pricey. For a low-cost alternative, hit the food court in Union Station (see p79), or the cafeteria at the Capitol Visitor Center (see p13). Better yet, pack a lunch and enjoy it on the Mall.

4 Plan your trip to cover a weekend. On weekends hotel room rates can be as little as half the weekday rates.

5 Look for a hotel that offers a robust free breakfast. It saves you time and the cost of a meal.

6 If you have a car with you, buy your gas outside DC, where it is much cheaper.

7 Hotels are also often cheaper in nearby Virginia and Maryland.

8 Check online private rental sites like VRBO (vrbo.com) and Airbnb (airbnb.com). It is possible to find a quality apartment or condominium in a great neighborhood for the about the same price as a discount hotel room.

9 Todaytix.com sells tickets to a variety of theater, dance and musical performances throughout the city.

10 Check websites and call those attractions that charge admission. They often offer discounts at specific times, or give out coupons that lower admission fees.

🔟 Festivals and Cultural Events

Chinese New Year celebrations

① Chinese New Year
MAP Q3 ■ Chinatown ■ Late Jan–early Feb

Lunar New Year is celebrated on a Sunday with special menus at the restaurants, traditional events, a parade, and fireworks. Simply pass through the ornate arch at 7th and H streets, NW to join in the colorful festivities.

② National Cherry Blossom Festival
MAP N6 ■ Tidal Basin ■ Late Mar–mid-Apr

The lake is surrounded by beautiful Japanese cherry trees, which originated with the 1912 gift of 3,000 specimens to the city by the mayor of Tokyo. The festival celebrating their spring blossoming includes a parade, performances, and offbeat but appropriate events as a sushi-making contest.

③ Filmfest DC
Citywide ■ Late Apr–early May ■ www.filmfestdc.org

This top-quality festival has brought the best of world cinema to the city since 1986. The most exciting new films are shown over two weeks at various venues, and discussions and film-oriented events are held at theaters and cafés across town.

④ Washington Nationals
MAP E4 ■ 1500 S Capitol St, SE ■ 202 675 NATS ■ Apr–Oct ■ www.mlb.com/nationals

Big-league baseball returned to Washington in 2005 after a 30-year absence. The Washington Nationals fill the stands of the Nationals Park from April to October.

⑤ Capital Pride
Jun ■ www.capitalpride.org

The Capital Pride Alliance organizes a month-long series of events to celebrate DC's LGBTQ+ community. Highlights include the Colorful Pridemobile Parade, Pride Talks, and pool parties.

⑥ Capital Jazz Fest
Merriweather Post Pavilion, Columbia, MD ■ Early Jun ■ www.capitaljazz.com

This annual three-day festival of jazz and blues features national and international artists and bands.

⑦ Giant National Capitol Barbecue Battle
MAP P4 ■ Pennsylvania Ave ■ Late Jun ■ www.bbqindc.com

Pennsylvania Avenue is awash with the enticing smell of smoked pork during the annual National Capitol Barbecue Battle. Top barbecue restaurants and pit-masters from around DC and the

Delicious treats at the Barbecue Battle

nation gather to compete for $40,000 in prize money. Visitors get to stroll the five-block-long venue, sampling tasty dishes, enjoying music, cooking demonstrations, and children's activities.

⑧ Smithsonian Folklife Festival

MAP N5 ▪ National Mall ▪ Jun–Jul
Entertaining cookery, storytelling, craft-making, dancing, music, and art fill the National Mall for two weeks around Independence Day (July 4). This is one of the largest and best cultural events in the world.

⑨ National Book Festival

MAP Q3 ▪ Washington Convention Center ▪ Sep ▪ www.loc. gov/bookfest
Organized and sponsored by the Library of Congress, this festival is free and open to the public. Around 50 authors of fiction, non-fiction, and children's books give readings, presentations, interviews, and book signings; plus, there are giveaways, promotions, and activities sponsored by leading publishing companies.

Visitors at the National Book Festival

⑩ Washington National Cathedral Christmas Services

MAP H4 ▪ Massachusetts & Wisconsin Aves, NW ▪ Dec ▪ Adm (some events); check website ▪ www.cathedral.org
The cathedral (see pp30–31) launches the festivities with Handel's Messiah concerts and stunning decorations. Throughout the season, music and concerts are presented, culminating with the elaborate celebrations of Christmas Eve and Christmas Day.

TOP 10 ONE-DAY EVENTS

Blossom Kite Festival

1 Martin Luther King, Jr. Day
Citywide ▪ 3rd Mon in Jan
Church services held. Check local papers for details.

2 President's Day
MAP D5 ▪ 3rd Mon in Feb
Alexandria, VA (see p111) hosts the nation's largest President's Day Parade, and Mount Vernon (see pp36–9) has free admission.

3 St. Patrick's Day
MAP Q4 ▪ Constitution Ave, NW ▪ Sun before Mar 17
A parade in honor of St. Patrick's Day.

4 Blossom Kite Festival
MAP N5 ▪ National Mall ▪ Late Mar/ early Apr
Competitions include home-built kites, fighting kites, and others.

5 White House Easter Egg Roll
MAP N4 ▪ White House ▪ Easter Mon
Children's activities, music, and egg rolling. Advance tickets only.

6 Memorial Day
Citywide ▪ Last Mon in May
Concerts, ceremonies and a parade on Constitution Avenue honor those who died in the service of their country.

7 Independence Day
MAP N5 ▪ National Mall ▪ Jul 4
The celebration culminates with a musical fireworks display.

8 National Symphony Labor Day Concert
MAP R5 ▪ US Capitol ▪ Labor Day
The official end of summer.

9 International Gold Cup Steeplechase Races
Great Meadows Events Centers, The Plains, VA ▪ Mid-Oct
Races at the peak of the fall foliage.

10 National Christmas Tree Lighting
MAP N4 ▪ The Ellipse ▪ Early Dec
The decorations are joyous.

🔟 Trips from Washington, DC

Vibrant fall colors on the mountains along Skyline Drive, Virginia

1 Baltimore, Maryland
Rte I-95 ■ Fort McHenry: 2400 East Fort Ave; open 9am–5:45pm daily; adm; www.nps.gov/fomc

Known as "Charm City", Baltimore offers museums of art, industry, baseball, marine trade science, and railroads along with historic sites from every American period. The city is also home to Fort McHenry, which inspired "The Star-Spangled Banner," the US national anthem, and Lexington Market, with over 100 food vendors.

2 Annapolis, Maryland
Rte 50 ■ William Paca House: 186 Prince George St; open 10am–5pm Mon–Sat, 11am–4pm Sun; closed Jan–late Mar; adm

One of the East Coast's sailing centers, Annapolis is home to the US Naval Academy. The main attractions here are the 18th-century home of William Paca, who was later the governor of Maryland, and the State Capitol.

A historical house in Annapolis

3 Skyline Drive, Virginia
Off Rte I-66 ■ Shenandoah National Park: adm; www.nps.gov/shen

This winding road passes 107 miles (170 km) through the mountain and valley scenery of Virginia's Shenandoah National Park. Hiking trails to isolated peaks, waterfalls, and rare forest environments begin from the main highway.

4 Harpers Ferry, West Virginia
Rte 340 ■ www.nps.gov/hafe

Before the Civil War, John Brown carried out his famous raid against government troops here, protesting the legality of slavery. This picturesque little town around the old Potomac waterfront has been well preserved and is filled with historic exhibits.

5 Chincoteague and Assateague, Virginia
Off Rte 13 ■ Chincoteague National Wildlife Refuge: 8231 Beach Rd; open sunrise–dusk daily

Best known for its wild ponies, Assateague Island offers activities, such as hiking, cycling, swimming, horseback riding, and kayaking.. The Chincoteague National Wildlife Refuge, spread across 22 sq miles (57 sq km), is a paradise for bird-watchers and nature buffs. The local seafood is first-rate, and the ice cream made here is justifiably famous.

6 Manassas Battlefield

Off Rte I-66 ■ National Battlefield Park: 6511 Sudley Rd; open dawn–dusk daily; www.nps.gov/mana

Two Civil War battles were fought here, where Union and Confederate soldiers fell by the thousands fighting for conflicting visions of the nation's future.

Ruins of a church in Jamestowne

7 Fredericksburg, Virginia

Rte 1 ■ Fredericksburg Walking Tour: 706 Caroline St; 540-373-1776; www.visitfred.com

This city has colonial homes, Civil War sites, and a downtown with shops and restaurants. A marked walking tour lays out milestones in the city's history.

8 Frederick, Maryland

Rte I-270 ■ Museum of Frederick County History: 24 E Church St; 301-663-1188; open 10am–4pm Tue–Sat; adm; www.frederick history.org

Noted for its bridges, this city is steeped in the memory of 19th-century life and Civil War battles. The downtown area was restored, and is now home to many antique dealers.

Gettysburg statue

9 Colonial Williamsburg and Historic Jamestowne

Off Rte 1-95 S ■ Colonial Williamsburg: open 9am–5pm daily; adm ■ Historic Jamestowne: open 9am–5pm daily; adm

Capital of the United States during the Revolutionary War, this city is the largest living history museum in America today. Nearby, Jamestown is a reconstruction of the first successful English settlement in America.

10 Gettysburg, Pennsylvania

Rte 15 ■ Gettysburg National Military Park: 1195 Baltimore Pike; 717-334-1124; open Apr-Oct: 6am-10pm daily (Nov-Mar: until 7pm)

The battle of Gettysburg in 1863 was the bloodiest of the Civil War. The Gettysburg National Military Park is one of the most visited sites.

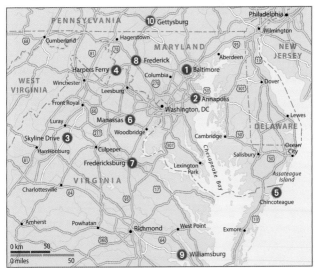

Washington, DC
Area by Area

Colorful townhouses in Georgetown

Around Capitol Hill	**78**
The National Mall	**84**
Penn Quarter	**94**
The White House and Foggy Bottom	**98**
Georgetown	**104**
Beyond the City Center	**110**

🔟 Around Capitol Hill

Folger Shakespeare Library and Theatre

Buzzing with the business of government, Capitol Hill is also a place for shopping, entertainment, food and drink, or simply strolling its handsome neighborhood streets. Approached from the west, the area begins with the landscaped US Capitol complex, which, as well as the Capitol itself, includes the US Botanic Garden, the Supreme Court Building, and the Library of Congress. Union Station, to the north, is one of the finest railroad terminals in the world.

AROUND CAPITOL HILL

① US Capitol

Symbolizing both government power and the control of that power by the people, the Capitol *(see pp12–15)* crowns the east end of the Mall.

② Union Station

MAP R4 ■ 50 Massachusetts Ave, NE

Opened in 1907, this magnificent Beaux Arts building is still a fully functional transportation hub. The lofty barrel-vaulted concourse, decorated with 70 lbs (32 kg) of gleaming gold leaf, is one of the great public spaces in the city – the Washington Monument, laid

Union Station's magnificent interior

on its side, would easily fit within its length. Over 23 million people pass through the station each year.

③ Folger Shakespeare Library and Theatre

MAP S5 ■ 201 East Capitol St, SE ■ 202-544-4600 ■ Closed for renovation ■ www.folger.edu

The world's largest library of printed editions of Shakespeare's works is at the Folger *(see p66)*, and performances at the 16th-century-style theater provide insights into Shakespeare and his times. There is also a huge collection of Renaissance works in other fields, plus playbills, musical instruments, and costumes. The library will be closed until 2023 for major renovations; check the website for performances and programs.

④ Library of Congress

MAP S5 ■ 101 Independence Ave, SE ■ 202-707-5000 ■ Opening hours vary, check website ■ www.loc.gov

The largest collection of books, recordings, and images in the world got its humble start when the US government bought 6,487 books from Thomas Jefferson after fire destroyed the first congressional library in 1814. Free hour-long tours of the spectacular Jefferson Building take in the Italianate-pillared Great Hall; the vast, circular Main Reading Room; a rare Gutenberg Bible; and Jefferson's original book collection.

1 Top 10 Sights
see pp79–81

① Places to Eat
see p83

① The Best of the Rest
see p82

5 Supreme Court Building

MAP S5 ■ 1st St & East Capitol St, NE ■ 202-479-3030 ■ Open 9am–4:30pm Mon–Fri; closed federal holidays ■ www.supremecourt.gov

The home of the highest seat of the judicial branch of the US government is a Neo-Classical building designed by Cass Gilbert – the American architect who designed the Woolworth Building in New York City. On its west pediment, above the main entrance's marble columns, is inscribed in bold letters the famous motto "Equal Justice Under Law."

6 Eastern Market

MAP S5 ■ 7th St & C St, SE ■ Open 8am–6pm Tue–Sat (to 5pm Sun) ■ www.easternmarket-dc.org

Completed in 1873, Eastern Market was designed by a prominent local architect, Adolph Cluss. Since then, it has served as a neighborhood meeting place and as a fresh food market with produce, cheese, meat, and fish. A variety of prepared food vendors are also popular. On weekends hundreds of local artists and crafters set up booths on the plaza.

7 Bartholdi Park and Fountain

MAP R5 ■ 1st St & Washington Ave, SW ■ www.usbg.gov

This park (see p59) is bursting with flowers and ornamental plants. Its symmetrical design radiates out from the fine Gilded Age

Bartholdi Park and Fountain

CAPITOL HILL RESIDENCES

In the early 19th century, the area east of the Capitol was filled with a motley collection of boarding houses and taverns where members of Congress stayed during legislative sessions. During the 19th and into the 20th centuries, a diverse mix of housing styles – Federal townhouses, manor houses, Queen Anne, interspersed with two-storey frame dwellings – developed. The protected Capitol Hill Historic District is now the largest historic residential district in the city.

---

cast-iron Bartholdi Fountain, a three-storey-high construction of supple human forms, European-style lights, and a non-stop flow of water.

8 US Botanic Garden

MAP R5 ■ On the Capitol grounds at Maryland Ave & 1st St, SW ■ 202-225-8333 ■ Garden: open 7:30am–5pm daily ■ Conservatory: open 10am–5pm daily ■ www.usbg.gov

Long valued by Capitol Hill residents as a quiet retreat, the Botanic Garden Conservatory (see p58) is home to some 4,000 living plants that have been arranged into themes and bio-systems, such as Plant Adaptations, Tropics, Orchids, and Medicinal Plants. The wedge-shaped National Garden, to the west of the Conservatory, includes glorious colorful outdoor displays. The main court is a wonderfully fragrant spot and a perfect place to sit and rest, and there's a Children's Garden to keep youngsters happy.

Exhibits at National Postal Museum

⑨ National Postal Museum

MAP R4 ▪ 2 Massachusetts Ave, NE ▪ Open 10am–5:30pm daily; closed Dec 25 ▪ postalmuseum.si.edu

The United States Postal Service (USPS) delivers over 500 million items of mail every day, and this fun museum *(see p62)* traces its development from the days of the Pony Express onwards.

⑩ Belmont-Paul Women's Equality National Monument

MAP S4 ▪ 144 Constitution Ave, NE ▪ 202-543-2240 ▪ Open 9am–5pm Wed–Sun; tours 9:30am, 11am, 2pm & 3:30pm ▪ Donation

Built in 1750 and expanded in 1800, this house *(see p49)* is one of the most historic in Washington. It was the only private residence burned during the War of 1812 *(see p42)* because Americans fired on the invading British from here. The completely rebuilt house was bought by the National Women's Party in 1929, and served as its headquarters until 2020 when the party dissolved. Visitors can see the period furnishings, objects and documents fundamental to the suffragist and feminist movements. In 2016 the house was designated as a US National Monument.

A DAY AROUND EASTERN MARKET

Folger Shakespeare Library and Theatre
Library of Congress
The Market Lunch
Eastern Market
The Flea Market at Eastern Market
Woven History and Silk Road
Eastern Market Metro Station

▶ MORNING

Before a day of shopping, begin with a bit of history at the **Library of Congress** *(see p79)*, a handsome example of the Italian Renaissance style, with unsurpassed interiors. Check the website for details on tour timings.

Turn right onto First Street, then right on East Capitol, and continue one block to the **Folger Shakespeare Library and Theatre** *(see p79)*. The Elizabethan theater is enchanting, and the materials on display are both rare and fascinating, as are the changing temporary exhibitions.

Walk east to 7th Street and turn right. A little over two blocks farther on is **Eastern Market**. On weekends, it is surrounded by arts and crafts vendors and flower stalls. **The Market Lunch** *(see p83)* inside is a great choice for a bite to eat and a rest.

AFTERNOON

If it's a Sunday, spend the afternoon at The Flea Market at Eastern Market, on 7th Street between C and Pennsylvania. It features 100 or more vendors selling antiques, Oriental rugs, fabrics, fine art photographs, jewelry, and other items. If the flea market is closed, walk a block south of Eastern Market and visit **Woven History and Silk Road** *(311–5 7th St, SE; 202-543-1705; open 11am–5pm Wed–Sun)* for its fabrics, rugs, and crafts from Asia and South America.

From here it's a short walk to Barracks Row, a historic street of boutique shops. Stop for dinner at one of the many restaurants here.

See map on pp78–9

The Best of the Rest

Capitol Grounds
MAP R4–R5

The lovely gardens and walkways that surround the Capitol are the work of renowned landscape designer Frederick Law Olmsted, who created the plan for the grounds in 1874.

Ebenezer United Methodist Church
MAP S5 ■ 400 D St, SE ■ Open 10am–2pm Mon–Fri

Washington's first congregation of African American Methodists and Episcopals. It also became home to the first public school for Black children after the Emancipation Proclamation.

Alleys and Carriageways
MAP S5

The alleys of Capitol Hill, notorious in the 19th century for their squalid and cramped houses, have today been turned into charming little homes.

Emancipation Monument
Lincoln Park ■ Metro Eastern Market

Lincoln Park (see p47) holds the Emancipation Proclamation while the last enslaved person, Archer Alexander, breaks his chains.

Robert A. Taft Memorial
MAP R4 ■ Constitution Ave & 1st St, NW ■ 202-226-8000 ■ Open 24 hrs daily

This memorial opposite the Capitol honors Senator Taft for his honesty and courage. The carillon in the 100-ft- (30-m-) tall bell tower plays every 15 minutes.

Statue of Mary McLeod Bethune
Lincoln Park ■ Metro Eastern Market

This modern sculpture shows the African American educator and activist (see p47) with two African American children. It symbolizes knowledge handed down through generations.

Christ Church
MAP S6 ■ 620 G St, SE

Built in 1805, this church had prominent parishioners, including presidents Jefferson, Madison, and Monroe.

National Guard Memorial Museum
MAP R4 ■ 1 Massachusetts Ave, NW ■ 202-789-0031 ■ Open 9am–4pm Mon–Fri ■ www.ngef.org

This gallery remembers citizens who gave their lives to protect the nation.

American Veterans Disabled for Life Memorial
MAP R5 ■ 150 Washington Ave, SW

This plaza-like oasis is dedicated to disabled veterans. It features a tree-shaded, star-shaped pool and interpretive glass and bronze panels.

Ulysses S. Grant Memorial
MAP R5 ■ US Capitol

This equestrian grouping honors the Union victory in the Civil War. Sculptor Henry Shrady (1871–1922) took 20 years to complete the work (see p51).

Sculpture of Mary McLeod Bethune

Places to Eat

PRICE CATEGORIES
For a three-course meal for one with half a bottle of wine (or equivalent meal), taxes and other charges.

$ under $50 $$ $50–100 $$$ over $100

A table at the Monocle

1 Dubliner Restaurant
MAP R4 ■ 4 F St, NW ■ 202-737-3773 ■ $$

An Irish pub with free-flowing pints and good hearty food, the Dubliner serves good steak and shepherd's pie. There is live Irish music from 8pm and the outdoor patio is perfect for warm summer evenings.

2 The Market Lunch
MAP S5 ■ Eastern Market, 225 7th St, SE ■ 202-547-8444 ■ No credit cards ■ $

This breakfast and lunch counter, with nearby tables, serves burgers and sandwiches, with a specialty in seafood. Try the crabcakes and oyster sandwiches. Breakfast and weekend brunch are very popular. Alcohol is not served here.

3 Café Berlin
MAP S4 ■ 322 Massachusetts Ave, NE ■ 202-543-7656 ■ $

A German restaurant in a townhouse setting. Café Berlin offers *Wiener schnitzel*, pork loin with sauerkraut, and other hearty dishes are on the menu. The desserts are very tempting.

4 Shake Shack
MAP R5 ■ 50 Massachusetts Ave, NE ■ 202-684-2428 ■ $

Located in Union Station's West Hall, this popular restaurant serves breakfast as well as a selection of burgers, hot dogs, fries, and shakes.

5 The Monocle
MAP S4 ■ 107 D St, NE ■ 202-546-4488 ■ $$

The Monocle claims to be the first fine-dining restaurant on Capitol Hill. Once a favorite dining spot of the Kennedys, it's still popular with the power-dining crowd and is known for its marbled steaks and ocean-fresh seafood.

6 Ambar
MAP S5 ■ 523 8th St, SE ■ 202-813-3039 ■ $$

Traditional yet modern Balkan fare is served here with an eclectic variety of small plates and East European wines.

7 Le Pain Quotidien
MAP S5 ■ 660 Pennsylvania Ave, SE ■ 202-459-9147 ■ $

A branch of the ubiquitous Belgian chain of light bite bakery cafés – the name means "daily bread."

8 Bistro Bis
MAP R4 ■ 15 E St, NW ■ 202-661-2700 ■ $

A modern take on a French bistro with a stylish cherry-wood interior; deservedly Bistro Bis is popular.

9 Tortilla Coast
MAP R5 ■ 400 1st St, SE ■ 202-546-6768 ■ $

Come here for some great Tex-Mex food. George W. Bush was a customer here before he was elected president.

10 Sonoma
MAP S5 ■ 223 Pennsylvania Ave, SE ■ 202-544-8088 ■ $

California cuisine, cheese platters, and an eclectic list of wines are the main draws at Sonoma.

See map on pp78–9

TOP 10 The National Mall

Even Washingtonians whose daily life rarely takes them to the National Mall regard this magnificent grassy park as the heart of the city. As it was visualized by Pierre Charles L'Enfant in his original plan for Washington, DC, it stretches 2.5 miles (4 km) from the Capitol to the Potomac River, just beyond the Lincoln Memorial. Alongside and nearby are key symbols of the city and the nation: memorials to past suffering and triumphs, the workplaces of the federal government, and the Smithsonian museums. The National Mall also serves as a national public square – it fills to capacity for the dazzling Fourth of July fireworks, and bustles daily with locals jogging, strolling, or just enjoying the extraordinary views.

National Museum of American History

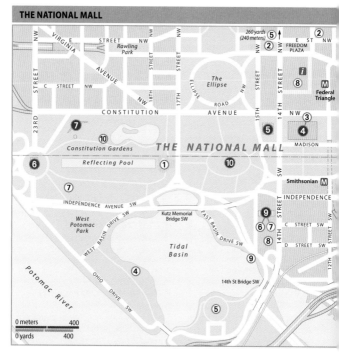

THE NATIONAL MALL

1 National Gallery of Art

Stroll through this building (see pp24–7) surrounded by illustrious artworks dating from before the Renaissance to the current day. The sculpture garden is a hit for its outdoor setting, summer jazz concerts, a winter ice-skating rink, and café.

2 National Museum of the American Indian

MAP Q5 ▪ 4th St at Independence Ave, SW ▪ Open 10am–5:30pm Tue–Sun; closed Dec 25

This museum (see p54) enshrines 10,000 years of American Indian life and culture, and acknowledges the place of Indigenous peoples in the history of the Americas. The collection features over 800,000 items, 7,000 of which are on display. Exhibits include pre-Columbian gold figurines, beadwork, textiles, and pottery from the Arctic to Patagonia. The building itself has been designed

The modern exterior of the National Museum of the American Indian

in harmony with American Indian beliefs. The National Native American Veterans Memorial opened in 2020 in the grounds of the museum. It honors the Native Americans who served in the US military.

3 National Air and Space Museum

The story of flight, one of the most stirring in human history, is powerfully depicted in this favorite museum (see pp20–21), renowned for its collection of precious artifacts of the challenging experience of flying.

4 National Museum of American History

The story of the United States of America, from its beginnings to the present day, is told here (see pp22–3) through public icons and examinations of the daily lives of ordinary people. The many exhibits include Julia Child's TV kitchen; Inventing in America; the Star-Spangled Banner Gallery; and "America on the Move," looking at modes of transport from 1876 to today.

5 National Museum of African American History and Culture

Opened in 2016, this vast museum (see pp32–3) explores African American history and culture in three core sections: History, Culture, and Community. The underground history galleries begin with Africa and the slave trade in the 1400s, detailing all the main events of African American history till present day. These galleries are complemented by exhibits on African American music, art, sports, and more on the upper floors.

1 Top 10 Sights
see pp85–7

1 Lunch Spots
see p91

1 The Best of the Rest
see p88

1 Children's Attractions
see p90

The magnificent Lincoln Memorial and Reflecting Pool

6 Lincoln Memorial

MAP M5 ■ 23rd St, NW & Independence Ave ■ Open 24 hours

This imposing marble memorial (see p50) honors the US president who shepherded the country through its most difficult era. Designed by Henry Bacon (1866–1924) and featuring a monumental 19-ft- (6-m-) high statue of the seated Lincoln by Daniel Chester French (1850–1931), the memorial was dedicated in 1922. The Greek architecture reflects the ideals of its time.

7 Vietnam Veterans Memorial

MAP M5 ■ Constitution Ave & 21st St, NW ■ Open 24 hours

This stark memorial (see p50) features a black polished wall on which are inscribed the names of those who died during the Vietnam War. Controversial when it was opened, because of its minimalism and unadorned black color, the memorial has become one of the most popular in the world. Its creator, the Chinese-American Maya Lin, was a 21-year-old student when she designed it. More traditional statues were added in 1984.

Statue at Vietnam Veterans Memorial

THE EISENHOWER MEMORIAL

Opened in 2020, this memorial honors Dwight D. Eisenhower, who served as the 34th US president from 1953 to 1961. The memorial was designed by Frank Gehry and sculptor Sergey Eylanbekov who created the bronze statues of Eisenhower. The entire memorial is backed by a mesh tapestry depicting the site of the Normandy landings in 1944, arguably Eisenhower's finest hour – he served as Supreme Commander of the Allied Forces in Europe during World War II.

8 National Museum of Natural History

A favorite with children, yet filled with fascinating displays and artifacts that appeal to everyone, the vast halls of this Smithsonian museum (see pp28–9) have everything from the tiny bones of a snake to a giant ritual statue from Easter Island. Other exhibits include the vast Mammal Hall, Pacific Island canoes, fabulous gemstones (such as the Hope Diamond), a giant squid, a set from a Chinese opera, and an Egyptian mummy case.

9 United States Holocaust Memorial Museum

MAP P5 ■ 100 Raoul Wallenberg Place, SW (14th St between C St & Independence Ave) ■ 202-488-0400 ■ Open 10am–5:30pm daily; closed Yom Kippur, Dec 25 ■ www.ushmm.org

Among the city's most harrowing sites, this museum (see pp54–5) is both a working study center for issues relating to the Holocaust and a national memorial for the millions murdered by the World War II Nazi government. The museum is solemn and respectful yet engrossing and highly informative. Free timed passes are required, from March to September, to view the three-storey permanent exhibition. Passes can be obtained at the museum on the day of visit, or in advance online. There are some special exhibitions that can be seen without passes.

⑩ Washington Monument

MAP P5 ■ 15th St between Independence & Constitution Aves ■ Open 9am–5pm daily (summer: until 10pm) ■ Entry by timed ticket

The plain Egyptian design of this radiant spire was largely the result of congressional cost-cutting, but now it seems an inspired choice. At 555 ft (165 m), the monument (see p50), built to honor the first president of the United States, towers over everything in the neighborhood and is ringed by 50 flags representing the 50 states of America. As a result of damage caused by a 5.8-magnitude earthquake in August 2011, the monument was closed for 32 months, reopening in May 2014. Visitors can now once more ascend by elevator to the 500-ft- (152-m-) high viewing deck for breathtaking views over the city.

The imposing Washington Monument

A MORNING WALK BY THE WATERFRONT

● Begin your walk at the **Franklin D. Roosevelt Memorial** (see p50) on West Basin Drive. There are hop-on-hop-off tour bus and trolley stops (see p124) directly in front (parking is limited). The sweep of this memorial carries visitors past waterscapes punctuated by engravings of the words of the president and evocative sculptures of his times.

On the left, leaving the memorial, is the little Japanese pagoda given to the city as a gesture of friendship by the mayor of Yokohama in 1958. Graceful Japanese cherry trees line the Tidal Basin bank beyond. Continue east across Inlet Bridge. About five minutes along the walkway stands the brilliant **Jefferson Memorial** (see p88), noted for its delicate design in spite of its size. Looking out from the steps here to the city is a wonderful experience.

Continue around the waterfront, cross Outlet Bridge, and bear to the left to the little boathouse, where you can rent paddle boats for a unique view of the Tidal Basin (open 10am–6pm daily; last boats out at 5pm; adm). If you prefer to stay on dry land, continue north toward the **Washington Monument** and cross Maine Avenue leading to Raoul Wallenberg Place. On the right is the **United States Holocaust Memorial Museum**. Before taking in the exhibits, gird yourself with some kosher fare in the **Museum Café** (see p91). Then spend the afternoon in remembrance of lives tragically lost under the Nazi regime before and during World War II.

See map on pp84–5

The Best of the Rest

The somber World War II Memorial

1 World War II Memorial
MAP N5 ▪ National Mall

This memorial *(see p51)* includes 12 bas-relief sculptures depicting America at war.

2 National World War I Memorial
MAP P4 ▪ 15th St, NW & Pennsylvania Ave, NW ▪ Open dawn–dusk daily

Opened in 2021, in a landscaped park previously known as Pershing Park, this memorial features a massive bronze sculpture dubbed *A Soldier's Journey*.

3 National Archives of the United States
MAP Q4 ▪ 700 Pennsylvania Ave, NW ▪ 866-272-6272 ▪ Open 10am–5:30pm daily

Home to foundation documents of the nation *(see p55)*, including the Declaration of Independence.

4 Franklin D. Roosevelt Memorial
MAP N6 ▪ 900 Ohio Dr, SW

The monument *(see p50)* depicts events during the Great Depression and World War II while FDR served as president.

5 Jefferson Memorial
MAP N6 ▪ Tidal Basin

Words taken from the Declaration of Independence are engraved on the wall here *(see p50)*.

6 International Spy Museum
MAP Q5 ▪ 700 L'Enfant Plaza, SW ▪ Open 9am–7pm Mon–Thu (to 8pm Fri–Sun) ▪ www.spymuseum.org

The Spy Museum *(see p65)* encourages visitors to adopt a cover identity and learn how to react to real espionage challenges using interactive displays.

7 Korean War Veterans Memorial
MAP M5 ▪ Daniel Chester French Dr & Independence Ave, SW

The 19 steel sculptures in this memorial to the 1953 Korean "police action" evoke the realities of war.

8 Bureau of Engraving and Printing
MAP P5 ▪ 14th St at C St, SW ▪ 202-874-2330 ▪ www.money factory.gov for tour info

See millions of dollars being printed as you walk along the gallery.

9 National Museum of African Art
MAP Q5 ▪ 950 Independence Ave, SW ▪ Open 10am–5:30pm daily; closed Dec 25

A program of changing exhibitions highlights a diverse collection of African pieces *(see p57)*.

10 Constitution Gardens
MAP N5 ▪ National Mall

This 50-acre (20-ha) park's lovely centerpiece is an island in a tranquil lake, where markers honor the 56 signers of the US Constitution.

The lush Constitution Gardens

Items in Museum Stores

1 American History Themes

The shops at the National Museum of American History *(see pp22–3)* offer a wide variety of merchandise inspired by museum exhibits. These include personalized dog tags, Star-Spangled Banner themed items, and pop-culture accessories.

2 Jackie Kennedy Jewels

Reproductions of Jackie's most famous pieces can be purchased for next to nothing at the museum store in the National Museum of American History *(see pp22–3)*.

3 All Things Dinosaur

You will find lots of dinosaur merchandise for sale, including the Smithsonian book *Dinosaur!*, in the National Museum of Natural History *(see pp28–9)*.

4 Geodes and Fossils

The Gem and Mineral store in the National Museum of Natural History *(see pp28–9)* has beautiful examples of geodes – sparkling crystals grown within hollows of other stones – and of fossils embedded in various matrixes.

5 Leather Flight Jackets

Good-quality leather jackets recreate the genuine flying jackets, and the selection and prices are reasonable. In the National Air and Space Museum *(see pp20–21)*.

6 American Indian Art

Sculptures, carvings, ceramic pots, and plates created in intricate American Indian designs can be purchased at the Museum of the American Indian *(see p85)*.

7 NASA Space Suits

Miniature orange suits, created with care and precise attention to detail, are available for little astronauts at the National Air and Space Museum *(see pp20–21)*.

Whistler's *Symphony in White, No. 1: The White Girl* in the National Gallery

8 National Gallery Prints

Many of the National Gallery's *(see pp24–7)* favorite paintings are available as quality prints, as well as in other forms ranging from phone cases to tote bags.

9 Cherry Blossom Kimono Jacket

Gorgeous satin kimono jackets and scarves are among the magnificent fabric creations available at DC's two fine Asian museum stores *(see p57)*. They also have unusual novelties such as a peacock jewelry box.

10 Handmade Crafts

The George Washington University Museum and the Textile Museum's *(see p99)* beautiful range of shawls and scarves, vibrant handbags, felt dolls, and inspiring textile-related books all make lovely gifts.

See map on pp84–5

🔟 Penn Quarter

Lincoln's carriage at Ford's Theatre

Like other urban downtown areas, Washington's city center is filled with shops, hotels, restaurants, and theaters for every taste. Yet downtown Washington borders Pennsylvania Avenue – often called "America's main street." This is the direct route between the White House and the Capitol, and is therefore, rich in historic associations. President Lincoln was shot in Ford's Theatre and died nearby; presidential inauguration parades sweep down the avenue every four years; citizens protest here. Washington's importance to world culture is reflected in the ease with which local restaurants and stores cater to an international clientele. The area draws visitors to the attractions of Chinatown, the Capital One Arena, and the feeling of being at the center of the political world.

PENN QUARTER

| ① | **Top 10 Sights** see pp95–6 |
| ① | **Places to Eat** see p97 |

The Great Hall of the National Building Museum

1 Ford's Theatre

MAP Q4 ■ 511 10th St, NW
■ 202-347-4833 ■ Open 9am–4:30pm
daily ■ Timed tickets; adm (advance
booking advised) ■ www.fords.org

John Wilkes Booth shot President
Abraham Lincoln in a balcony
box here on April 14,
1865 – a tragic
event that has
made Ford's
Theatre (see p66)
one of America's
best-known historical
sites. A museum contains Booth's
.44 caliber Derringer pistol and
other objects alongside interesting
information about President Lincoln
and the assassination plot. The
restored building also hosts theater
productions. Directly across
10th Street is Petersen House,
where Lincoln died after being
carried from the theater.

**Booth's
Derringer pistol**

2 National Building Museum

MAP Q4 ■ 401 F St, NW ■ Open
10am–5pm Mon–Sat, 11am–5pm
Sun ■ Adm ■ www.nbm.org

This grand structure would be a
fabulous place to visit even if it were
empty. Its eight massive interior
columns are among the largest in
the world, and its immense interior
space has beautiful natural light. The
museum is dedicated to documenting
and displaying themes in the art and
craft of building. It has permanent
exhibitions on Washington city and on
art created from tools, and mounts
temporary exhibitions on topics such
as the growth of urban transit and
the development of architectural and
construction methods. Other exhibits
highlight the work of individual prominent architects. Families with young
children will particularly enjoy
the Building Zone, where they
can build towers and drive
toy bulldozers.

3 Capital One Arena

MAP Q4 ■ 601 F St, NW

While the Capital One Arena (see
p67) is principally a sports arena,
it has also become an unofficial
community center. It's a popular
venue for college and professional
sports events, big-name concerts,
circuses, figure-skating performances, and other events.

4 Clara Barton Missing Soldiers Office Museum

MAP P4 ■ 437 7th St, NW ■ 202-824-
0613 ■ Open Wed–Sun for reserved
tours by appt only ■ Adm ■ www.
clarabarton museum.org

A battlefield nurse, Clara Barton,
established this military office that is
tucked inside a brick boarding house.
Along with her small staff, Miss
Barton dedicated her life to assisting
families who wished to locate their
loved ones lost at war. Today the
museum tells the incredible true
story of how more than 22,000 unac-
counted for soldiers were found,
following the end of the Civil War.

5 National Museum of Women in the Arts

MAP P3 ▪ 1250 New York Ave, NW ▪ 202-783-5000 ▪ Closed for renovation ▪ Adm ▪ www.nmwa.org

The collection of works by female artists here *(see p57)* is among the best in the world, and ranges from Italian artist Lavinia Fontana's *Portrait of a Noblewoman* (c1580) to Mexican artist Frida Kahlo's 1937 *Self-Portrait Dedicated to Leon Trotsky.*

6 Planet Word

MAP P3 ▪ 925 13th St, NW ▪ Open 10am–5pm Thu–Sun ▪ www.planetwordmuseum.org

Housed in the historic Franklin School, this museum celebrates language with voice-activated exhibits and interactive galleries. Displays here explore the origins of words and the diversity of languages. Visitors can paint a virtual wall, solve word puzzles, or sing karaoke.

7 Smithsonian American Art Museum

MAP Q4 ▪ 8th & F Sts, NW ▪ 202-633-7970 ▪ Open 11:30am–7pm daily; closed Dec 25 ▪ www.americanart.si.edu

This large and inclusive collection consists of works by a range of renowned American artists such as Georgia O'Keefe, Winslow Homer, John Singleton Copley, and many others. Exhibits include the "American Experience," "Art Since 1945," and "Graphic Arts."

Sculpture at the Smithsonian American Art Museum

8 Freedom Plaza

MAP P4 ▪ Pennsylvania Ave between 13th & 14th Sts, NW

A popular site for festivals and political protests, Freedom Plaza is located near the National Theatre *(see p67).* South of the plaza is the Beaux Arts District Buidling. Around the edge are engraved quotations about the city from President Wilson and Walt Witman, among others.

PENNSYLVANIA AVENUE

When the federal government moved to the city in 1800, Pennsylvania Avenue was selected as the "main street" because the area to the south was too muddy after rains, and the avenue offered a direct route from the President's House to the Capitol – at that time the only substantial buildings in town.

9 National Portrait Gallery

MAP Q4 ▪ 8th & F Sts, NW ▪ 202-633-8300 ▪ Open 11:30am–7pm daily ▪ www.nps.si.edu

The ornate 1836 building is a masterpiece in itself. The gallery *(see p56)* celebrates remarkable Americans through visual and per-forming arts. Exhibitions focus on individuals who have helped to shape the country's culture, from presidents and activists to villains and poets. The waved glass cover over the courtyard is by renowned architect Norman Foster.

10 Chinatown

MAP Q3 ▪ 7th & H Sts, NW

Although filled with modern bars, restau-rants, and shops today, this neighborhood still retains some vestiges of traditional Chinese culture. Look out for the Friendship Arch which marks the center, with even pagoda-style roofs ornamented with 300 dragons.

Friendship Arch in Chinatown

Places to Eat

PRICE CATEGORIES
For a three-course meal for one with half
a bottle of wine (or equivalent meal),
taxes and extra charges.

$ under $50 $$ $50–100 $$$ over $100

1 Matchbox
MAP Q4 ■ 750 E St, NW
■ 202-289-4441 ■ $

Exposed tin ceilings, brick interiors and
vintage photographs give Matchbox
a cozy yet rustic vibe. The menu here
offers delicious comfort foods and
exceptional wood-fired pizza combos.

2 Jaleo
MAP Q4 ■ 480 7th St, NW
■ 202-628-7949 ■ $$

A fine tapas restaurant, Jaleo draws
rave reviews for its eggplant flan and
sautéed shrimp. The atmosphere is
always lively, with great music and
plenty of sangria.

3 Old Ebbitt Grill
MAP P3 ■ 675 15th St, NW
■ 202-347-4800 ■ $

Founded in 1856, this is the oldest
saloon in the city, serving great ham-
burgers and seasonal entrées. When
in season, sample the Oyster bar.

4 Rasika
MAP Q4 ■ 633 D St, NW
■ 202-637-1222 ■ $$$

With an elegant setting and beautiful
plating, Rasika (see p69) offers some
innovative dishes from Indian cuisine.
Done up by modernist curators, the
decor mirrors an Indian palace. Favorites include mango shrimp, and the
traditional chicken tikka masala.

5 Elephant and Castle
MAP P4 ■ 1201 Pennsylvania
Ave, NW ■ 202-347-7707 ■ $

Traditional British comfort food is
served here in a homey pub-style
atmosphere: the roast-beef-filled
Yorkshire puddings, sausage and
mash, and shepherd's pie are
among the perennial favorites.

Bright decor at Brasserie Beck

6 Brasserie Beck
MAP P3 ■ 1101 K St, NW
■ 202-408-1717 ■ $$

A paradise for beer-lovers, Beck
offers several varieties and a large
French–Belgian menu.

7 Full Kee
MAP Q3 ■ 509 H St, NW
■ 202-371-2233 ■ $

This popular Chinatown Cantonese
restaurant serves delicious soups
at an open station.

8 Oyamel Cocina Mexicana
MAP Q4 ■ 401 7th St, NW
■ 202-628-1005 ■ $$

Traditional antonjitos and great
cocktails at this Mexican spot.

9 Tony Cheng's Mongolian Restaurant
MAP Q3 ■ 619 H St, NW
■ 202-371-8669 ■ $

The ground floor of this restaurant
focuses on Mongolian-style barbecue while Cantonese cuisine
and dim sum are served upstairs.

10 District Chophouse and Brewery
MAP Q4 ■ 509 7th St, NW
■ 202-347-3434 ■ $$

Hearty, meaty menus and on-site
handcrafted ales cater to sports
fans from the Capital One Arena.

See map on p94

🔟 The White House and Foggy Bottom

Bust of JFK, Kennedy Center

The majestic White House clearly defines this part of the city – many government buildings stand in the vicinity, including the Federal Reserve Building, the old and new Executive Office Buildings, and the State and Treasury Departments. To the west lies Foggy Bottom, a former swamp area now home to George Washington University. Farther west, the Kennedy Center stands on the Potomac waterfront. The area is characterized by high-end restaurants, hotels, and shops, as well as a smattering of galleries, historic churches, and small museums.

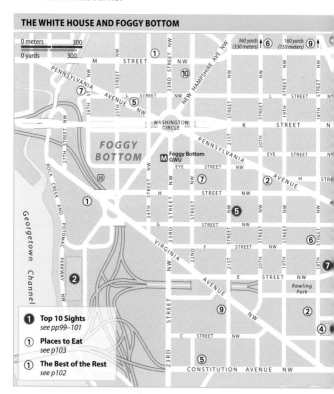

THE WHITE HOUSE AND FOGGY BOTTOM

FOGGY BOTTOM

Georgetown Channel

ROCK CREEK AND POTOMAC PARKWAY

WASHINGTON CIRCLE

Ⓜ Foggy Bottom GWU

Rawling Park

- ❶ **Top 10 Sights** see pp99–101
- ① **Places to Eat** see p103
- ① **The Best of the Rest** see p102

1 The White House

Beautiful from any angle, the White House (see pp16–19) is a symbol of US political power and of democracy throughout the world.

2 Kennedy Center

MAP M4 ■ 2700 F St, NW ■ 202-467-4600

A memorial to President John F. Kennedy, this massive performance complex – the largest in the country – presents the very best expressions of the artistic culture he loved so well. Here (see p66), national and international stars present performances of opera, classical music, musical comedy, drama, jazz, dance, and ballet. Located overlooking the Potomac, its terraces and rooftop restaurant offer spectacular views of the city below.

3 St. John's Church

MAP N3 ■ 1525 H St, NW ■ Open 9am–3pm Mon–Sat ■ Tours after the Sunday service (summer: 10:30am, winter: 11am) ■ www.st johns-dc.org

This lovely yellow Episcopalian Church, located on the north side of Lafayette Square, was designed by Benjamin Latrobe and conducted its first service in 1816. From James Madison to Joe Biden, every president of the United States has attended a service at St. John's. The cast iron bell in the steeple was cast by Joseph Revere, son of the American Revolution patriot Paul, in 1822. The 25 stained-glass windows, designed and created by Lorin Stained Glass Windows of Chartres, France, were installed in 1885.

4 Renwick Gallery

MAP N3 ■ 1661 Pennsylvania Ave, NW ■ 202-633-7970 ■ Open 10am–5:30pm daily ■ www.renwick. americanart.si.edu

With its collections of fine American craft works and art, and having undergone extensive renovations, this Smithsonian museum (see p56) is a gem. The second-floor Grand Salon served as a ballroom and site for special events when the Corcoran Gallery was located here before 1897. Named after its architect, James Renwick, Jr., the 1859 structure is a marvelous Second Empire-style building.

5 The George Washington University Museum and The Textile Museum

MAP M3 ■ 21st and G St, NW ■ Opening times vary, check website ■ Adm ■ www.museum.gwu.edu

The museum includes the Albert H. Small Washingtoniana Collection of historic Washington, DC documents, and the Textile Museum Collection of over 20,000 objects spanning 5,000 years. The fine Islamic, Peruvian, Pre-Columbian, and Coptic textiles and Oriental carpets are recognized as one of the world's foremost specialized museum collections.

BLACK LIVES MATTER PLAZA

In 2020, DC Mayor Muriel Bowser renamed a section of 16th Street NW the "Black Lives Matter Plaza." This was done after the city and much of the country erupted in protest (**below**) at the murder of African American George Floyd by a white Minneapolis police officer. As part of the protests, members of the DC Public Works Department painted "Black Lives Matter" in yellow on 16th Street.

6 Treasury Building

MAP P4 ■ 1500 Pennsylvania Ave, NW ■ Tours only for citizens and legal residents of the US, pre-registration required, Sat am; check website ■ www.treasury.gov

The ornate Greek-Revival style of this building (see p49), designed in 1833, suggests a Temple of Money, and its imposing interior design confirms the seriousness with which the republic has always treated its currency. The restored Salmon P. Chase Suite and the Andrew Johnson Office reflect the gravity of official actions during and after the Civil War. The burglar-proof vault is always a hit with visitors, not least because of the beauty of its cast-iron walls and its demonstration of the lower security needs of a simpler time.

7 The Octagon Museum

MAP N4 ■ 1799 New York Ave, NW ■ 202-626-7439 ■ Open 1–4pm Thu–Sat ■ www.architects foundation.org

This unique and graceful building houses the oldest architecture museum in the country. It was designed by William Thornton, the original architect of the US Capitol Building, as a second home for John Tayloe III, a wealthy friend of George Washington. The house was completed in 1801 – one of the first private residences to be built to Pierre L'Enfant's plan – and provided shelter to President James Madison and his family while workers were rebuilding the White House after its destruction during the War of 1812. The exhibitions of the museum focus on the early Federal period of architecture, principally from 1800 to 1830.

8 Daughters of the American Revolution

MAP N4 ■ 1776 D St, NW ■ 202-628-1776 ■ Museum: open 8:30am–4pm Mon–Fri, 9am–5pm Sat; closed federal holidays ■ www.dar.org

The largest concert hall in the city is in Constitution Hall, the grand performance space operated by the Daughters of the American Revolution (DAR). The cornerstone of this John Russell Pope design was laid in 1928, using the same trowel George

Treasury Building

Washington used for the US Capitol building cornerstone in 1793. The DAR also contains a fascinating museum of early American artifacts, ranging from a simple 17th-century dwelling to an elaborate Victorian parlor. The DAR is also a volunteer women's service promoting patriotism, history, and education – any woman who can prove lineal descent from a patriot of the American Revolution is eligible to join.

9 Lafayette Park
MAP N3 ■ H St between 15th and 17th Sts, NW

In DC's early years, this park served as a racetrack, a zoo, a graveyard, and in 1812 it encamped soldiers during the war. Today, it overlooks the North Portico of the White House, making it a favorite spot for TV news broadcasts, protests and celebrations. The park and the neighboring buildings are a National Historic Landmark. Of its five statues, the central one is of US President Andrew Jackson on his horse. The others, located in the four corners of the park, are of foreign volunteers who fought in the Revolution, including France's General Marquis Gilbert de Lafayette.

Statue in Lafayette Park

10 National Geographic Museum
MAP N3 ■ 1145 17th & M Sts, NW ■ 202-857-7700 ■ Open 10am–6pm daily; closed Thanksgiving, Dec 25 ■ Adm ■ www.nationalgeographic.org/dc

The first-class exhibits at this museum (see p63) cover foreign cultures, nature, archeology, and *National Geographic*'s signature breathtaking photography. Displays immerse visitors in their subject matter, all reflecting the diversity of our ever-changing planet.

A DAY EXPLORING 17TH STREET, NW

> #### MORNING

Begin your day admiring the **St. John's Church** *(see p99)*. Next, walk west to **Decatur House** *(see p102)*, a Neo-Classical mansion. From here, turn left and walk to the end of the block; turn left onto 17th Street, NW, and continue one block to Pennsylvania Avenue. The **Renwick Gallery** *(see p99)* on the corner has a magnificent exterior and houses fascinating exhibits. Continuing east on Pennsylvania Avenue, you can view the renowned north portico of **The White House** *(see pp16–19)* on your right. Reverse direction, return to 17th Street, and turn left to take in the ornate **Eisenhower Executive Office Building** *(see p49)* and double back to grab a bite at **Equinox** *(see p103)*. After lunch head south to the Corcoran **School of the Arts and Design**, where Gallery 102 *(see p102)* hosts works by students and DC-area artists. Admire its wonderful Beaux Arts atrium.

AFTERNOON

After leaving the Corcoran, turn right and continue down 17th Street one block to D Street. Turn right, and almost at the end of the block you'll see the entrance of the **Daughters of the American Revolution**. In addition to its fascinating period rooms, its gift shop is a treat for anyone with an interest in historic reproductions or porcelain. End your day by hailing a taxi on 17th Street to the **Kennedy Center** *(see p99)* and enjoy dinner at the **Roof Terrace Restaurant** *(202-416-8555)*, which offers views of the Potomac River.

The Best of the Rest

1 Watergate Hotel
MAP M3 = 2650 Virginia Ave, NW = www.thewatergatehotel.com

This hotel achieved notoriety after a political scandal in 1972 that led to President Nixon's resignation. Stay at "The Scandal Room" 214.

Watergate Hotel with riverfront views

2 U.S. Department of the Interior Museum
MAP N4 = 1849 C St, NW = Open 8:30am–4:30pm Mon–Fri = www.doi.gov

A niche museum showcases the fascinating work and history of the US Department of the Interior.

3 Farragut Square
MAP N3 = 912 17th St, NW

Named after Admiral David Farragut, this green space hosts family-friendly events called "Farragut Fridays."

4 Art Museum of the Americas
MAP N4 = 201 18th St, NW = Open 10am–5pm Tue–Sun = www.museum.oas.org

An art museum focusing on modern and contemporary art from Latin America and the Caribbean.

5 Statue of Albert Einstein
MAP M4 = 2101 Constitution Ave, NW

Created by Robert Berks, this bronze statue of Albert Einstein (see p51) is set outside the National Academy of Sciences.

Bronze statue of Albert Einstein

6 DACOR Bacon House
MAP N4 = 1801 F St, NW = Tours 2:30–4:30pm Mon, Wed & Thu = www.dacorbacon.org

Built in 1825, this handsome Federal-style house now features the Ringgold-Marshall Museum of Diplomacy.

7 Gallery 102
MAP M3 = 801 22nd St, NW = Open 9am–5pm Mon–Fri = www.corcoran.gwu.edu

Set on the Corcoran School of the Arts and Design campus, this museum (see p101) exhibits contemporary art from the students and DC-area artists.

8 Decatur House
MAP N3 = 1610 H St, NW = 202-218-4300 = Tours 11am, 12:30pm & 2pm Mon

This townhouse (see p48) was built for Commodore Stephen Decatur and his wife Susan in 1818. It now houses the David M. Rubenstein National Center for White House History.

9 The National Museum of American Diplomacy
MAP M4 = 330 21st St, NW = Open 1–3pm Fri = www.diplomacy.state.gov

Set to open in 2022, this museum's galleries will document the history of American diplomacy. Until then visitors can view the preview exhibit "Diplomacy Is Our Mission."

10 Cathedral of St. Matthew the Apostle
MAP N2 = 1725 Rhode Island Ave, NW = Open 10am–2pm Mon–Fri, 7:30am–end of Mass Sat, 6:30am–7pm Sun = www.stmatthewscathedral.org

Completed in 1895, this grand Romanesque Revival-style church has lavish interiors featuring a huge mosaic of St. Matthew behind the main altar.

Places to Eat

PRICE CATEGORIES

For a three-course meal for one with half a bottle of wine (or equivalent meal), taxes and extra charges.

$ under $50 $$ $50–100 $$$ over $100

1 Blue Duck Tavern

MAP M3 ▪ 1201 24th St, NW ▪ 202-419-6755 ▪ $$

The chef's specialties are prepared before your eyes in an open kitchen at this restaurant (see p68). Must-try dishes include thick fries cooked in duck fat, braised beef rib, and the coconut tapioca dessert.

2 Founding Farmers

MAP N3 ▪ 1924 Pennsylvania Ave, NW ▪ 202-822-8783 ▪ $$

Both sustainable and stylish, this celebration of fresh food is brought to you by a collective of American family farmers.

3 Equinox

MAP N3 ▪ 818 Connecticut Ave, NW ▪ 202-331-8118 ▪ $$

A showplace for fresh local produce, Equinox also boasts a pioneer in modern American cooking, chef Todd Gray. The menu is seasonal and features many organic, sustainable ingredients.

Elegant interior of Equinox

4 Georgia Brown's

MAP P3 ▪ 950 15th St, NW ▪ 202-393-4499 ▪ $$

Southern cooking with very generous portions are served here. Try chicken, fish, stews, shrimp, and grits.

5 Marcel's

MAP M3 ▪ 2401 Pennsylvania Ave, NW ▪ 202-296-1166 ▪ $$$

Award-winning French and Belgian cuisine, including crispy skate wing and Carolina pheasant, wins rave reviews (see p69). There is a pre-theater menu available for $85.

6 Obelisk

MAP N2 ▪ 2029 P St, NW ▪ 202-872-1180 ▪ $$$

Experience fine dining with a comfortable ambience. Obelisk (see p68) serves five-course meals consisting of simple and innovative dishes.

7 La Perla

MAP M3 ▪ 2600 Pennsylvania Ave, NW ▪ 202-333-1767 ▪ $$$

Traditional Italian fare with a focus on pasta, seafood, wine, and desserts is on offer at La Perla.

8 Bua Thai Restaurant

MAP N2 ▪ 1635 P St, NW ▪ 202-265-0828 ▪ $

This Thai restaurant offers favorites such as papaya salad, pad thai, green curry, and sticky rice with mango.

9 Iron Gate

MAP N2 ▪ 1734 N St, NW ▪ 202-524-5202 ▪ $$

Borrowing from both Greek and Italian cuisines, Iron Gate (see p69) offers perfect Mediterranean setting with its leafy courtyard.

10 Westend Bistro

MAP M3 ▪ 1190 22nd St, NW ▪ 202-974-4900 ▪ $$

This spot (see p68) features happy hour specials on weekdays and a Sunday brunch stocked with comfort food favorites such as waffles.

See map on pp98–9

TOP 10 Georgetown

When Abigail Adams arrived in the city in 1800, she described Georgetown as "the very dirtiest hole I ever saw." It was then a major port with a huge slave and tobacco trade, cheap housing, and commercial wharves. But the Chesapeake and Ohio Canal and the Baltimore and Ohio Railroad brought prosperity to Georgetown, and therefore style. When the canal began to fail, the district went with it, until Franklin D. Roosevelt partly rehabilitated the area. It was back in the Kennedy era that Georgetown became the fashionable neighborhood it is today.

Fountain in Dumbarton Oaks

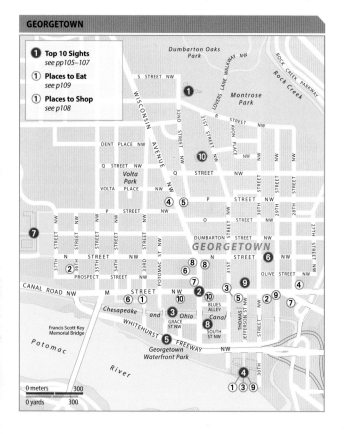

GEORGETOWN

① Top 10 Sights
see pp105–107

① Places to Eat
see p109

① Places to Shop
see p108

0 meters 300
0 yards 300

1 Dumbarton Oaks Museum and Gardens

MAP L1 ■ 1703 32nd St, NW ■ 202-339-6400 ■ Museum: open 11:30am–5:30pm Tue–Sun ■ Gardens: open Mar–Oct: 2–6pm Tue–Sun ■ Adm (gardens only)

This elegant Federal-style house, with its Philip Johnson-designed wing, houses a world-renowned collection of Byzantine and pre-Columbian artifacts. El Greco's *Visitation* is here also, possibly the Spanish master's last painting. The house and its museum *(see p49)* are enclosed by acres of delightful landscaping, including a charming rose garden, a sparkling fountain terrace, and an orangery *(see p59)*. In spring, this is one of the loveliest and most peaceful spots in the city to see cherry trees in blossom.

2 M Street and Wisconsin Avenue

MAP L3

This intersection is surrounded by the main shopping, entertainment, dining, and bar-crawling areas of Georgetown. The attractive shops include retailers of cool urban clothes, jewelry, fine wine, gourmet foods, art and antiques, and other specialties. Restaurant food of every description is available, from modern gourmet to casual eateries.

3 Chesapeake and Ohio Canal

MAP L3 ■ Georgetown Visitor Center: 1057 Thomas Jefferson St, NW; 301-739-4200; www.nps.gov/choh

The C&O Canal *(see p58)* grew from a dream of George Washington's as a gateway to commerce with the west ("west" meaning Ohio at the time). Coal, flour, fur, timber, whiskey, iron ore, and other goods traveled on barges, towed by mules walking along canalside paths. The canal's commercial days are over, but its entire length from Georgetown to Maryland has been turned into beloved National Parks

Boat tour, Chesapeake and Ohio Canal

in the region. You can experience the beauty and serenity of the canal by walking about a block south from M Street, NW, and turning west onto the canal's towpath. Then walk the lovely 1.5-mile- (2.5-km-) stretch to Abner Cloud House, where you can rent kayaks.

4 Washington Harbour

MAP L3 ■ 3000 K St, NW, at the bottom of Thomas Jefferson St, NW (between 30th & 31st Sts)

Good restaurants and dockside cafés; the water taxi terminal; the Thompson boathouse; lovely views of the Potomac River and the Kennedy Center; walkways for strolling and benches for resting – all of these attractions and more make the harbor a magnet for Georgetowners. As a bonus, in winter the fountain area transforms into DC's largest outdoor skating rink. On the west side, a riverfront walkway leads to the lush green paths and tree shaded benches of Georgetown Waterfront Park *(see p106)*.

The bustling Washington Harbour

5 Georgetown Waterfront Park

MAP L3 ■ Water St, NW ■ www.georgetownwaterfrontpark.org

This park runs along the Potomac between 31st and 34th Streets, NW towards Key Bridge. A large, interactive fountain delights children on hot days and broad stone steps lead down to the water's edge.

6 N Street

MAP L2

Little attractions and oddities abound on this street, which is noted for its exemplary architecture. At No. 2801 is the Kesher Israel Synagogue of Georgetown, founded by Eastern European immigrants. Author Herman Wouk and Senator Joseph Lieberman were both members. The elegant Federal house at No. 3038 was home to Ambassador Averell Harriman, who lent it to Jacqueline Kennedy after her husband's assassination. She later bought the 1794 Thomas Beall House across the street. Lessons in 19th-century architecture can be learned from the Federal houses at Nos. 3327 and 3339, the Second-Empire home at No. 3025–7, and the Victorian homes of Wheatley Row at Nos. 3041–45.

Facade of Georgetown University

its stone towers seemingly brooding with age. Yet the university is one of the most progressive in the country. Among the many interesting buildings here is the 1875 Healy Hall, built in an elaborate Flemish Renaissance style with surprising spiral adornment. Visitors can obtain campus maps and suggestions for strolls at Room 103, White-Gravenor Hall.

8 Grace Church

MAP L3 ■ 1041 Wisconsin Ave, NW ■ Church: open by appt; 202-333-7100; office: open 10am–6pm Mon, Tue & Fri

This 1866 church was built to house a congregation founded to serve the boatmen and support staff of the C&O

Buildings on N Street

7 Georgetown University

MAP G2 ■ White-Gravenor Hall, O & 37th Sts, NW ■ 202-687-0100 ■ Call for opening hours

Overlooking Georgetown and the Potomac, this venerable institution sits on a hill like a medieval citadel,

---

RIDE THE CIRCULATOR TO GEORGETOWN

Since Georgetown has no Metrorail station, it used to be difficult for visitors to get to the area's attractions. The big red buses of the DC Circulator now alleviate the problem, running daily every 10 minutes on two routes that provide cheap access to Georgetown. The first route connects Dupont Circle (19th and N Streets), Georgetown, and Rosslyn Metro station. The second route runs from Union Station to downtown Georgetown. Circulator buses *(see p119)* run between 7am and midnight and cost $1.

A MORNING IN GEORGETOWN

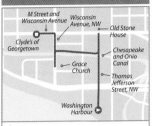

M Street and Wisconsin Avenue
Wisconsin Avenue, NW
Old Stone House
Clyde's of Georgetown
Chesapeake and Ohio Canal
Grace Church
Thomas Jefferson Street, NW
Washington Harbour

Canal. The simple but elegant design brings back the mid-19th century, without the raucous bustle that must have accompanied the canal at its peak. The grounds are peaceful and the church offers poetry readings, theater performances, and concerts.

⑨ Old Stone House
**MAP L2 ▪ 3051 M St, NW
▪ 202-426-6851 ▪ Open 11am–7pm daily ▪ www.nps.gov/rocr**

Dating from 1765, this residence looks a little incongruous in the heart of the shopping area, but provides a captivating window into 18th-century life. Today it serves as a visitor center for Rock Creek Park (see p59), with displays on the history of the house and its former owners.

⑩ Tudor Place
**MAP L2 ▪ 1644 31st St, NW
▪ 202-965-0400 ▪ Tours of the house: 10am–3pm Tue–Sat, noon–3pm Sun; gardens: open 10am–4pm Tue–Sat, noon–4pm Sun; closed Jan, federal holidays ▪ Adm**

This house-museum is remarkable for its beauty as well as its historic interest. Completed in 1816, it was built by Thomas Peter, son of a Georgetown tobacco merchant, and Martha Custis Peter, granddaughter of Martha Washington. The Peter family lived here for six generations and hosted many prominent guests.

Begin at **Washington Harbour** (see p105) for its views of the Potomac River right from the waterfront. Take a pleasant stroll along the river before heading up Thomas Jefferson Street, NW, to the Georgetown Visitor Center for the **Chesapeake and Ohio Canal** (see p105). Then turn right and continue up Thomas Jefferson Street for a short block and cross M Street, NW. In front of you is the **Old Stone House**. National Park Service interpreters recreate some of the daily activities that might have taken place in this old house in the 18th century.

Reverse direction and return down Thomas Jefferson Street to the canal. Turn right onto the towpath and stroll for two blocks until you reach an opening in the embankment. Follow the steps to the right to Wisconsin Avenue, NW. To the left is the lovely little Grace Church, built for the spiritual needs of workers on the canal. The grounds, with their mature trees, make a peaceful relaxation spot. Recross the canal and walk up to the shops at the intersection of **M Street and Wisconsin Avenue** (see p105).

Before an afternoon of retail therapy, turn left on M Street for lunch at the popular **Clyde's of Georgetown** (see p109), whose menu uses seasonal, local produce, or try one of the many side-street cafés.

Red door of Grace Church

Places to Shop

1 Intermix
MAP L3 ▪ 3300 M St, NW
▪ www.intermixonline.com
Shop luxury brands and upcoming fashion labels at this New York-based women's fashion chain. Consult the in-store stylists who can help you put together the perfect outfit.

2 Georgetown Olive Oil
MAP L3 ▪ 2910 M St, NW
▪ www.georgetownoliveoil.com
This local food store sells high-quality olive oils from Greece, Italy, and Spain. It also offers balsamic vinegars and luxury products, such as black truffle, sea salt, and Youthberry white tea.

3 Rothy's
MAP L3 ▪ 3068 M St, NW
▪ www.rothys.com
Specializing in classic footwear for men and women, this small eco-friendly chain creates its products with 100 per cent recycled materials. It offers comfortable shoes and carry-bags knit from repurposed plastic water bottles.

4 The Phoenix
MAP L2 ▪ 1514 Wisconsin Ave, NW
A charming, family-run store with contemporary clothing in natural fibers, classic jewelry, folk and fine art, unique items of homeware, and Mexican antiques.

5 Christ Child Society Opportunity Shop
MAP L2 ▪ 1427 Wisconsin Ave, NW
A treasure trove of antiques and collectibles, with proceeds going to charity. Best items upstairs.

6 Jewelers'Werk Galerie
MAP K3 ▪ 3319 Cadys Alley, NW
A showplace of handcrafted jewelry and wearable art, tucked away in Georgetown's Cadys Alley design enclave. The store is stocked with intricate necklaces, earrings, and brooches by artists and designers.

Vibrant display at Bridge Street Books

7 Bridge Street Books
MAP L3 ▪ 2814 Pennsylvania Ave, NW
Georgetown has few dedicated bookstores – this narrow, two-storey townhouse is fertile ground for anyone with a serious interest in history, literature, film, politics, philosophy, cultural studies, or poetry.

8 John Fluevog Shoes
MAP L2 ▪ 1265 Wisconsin Ave, NW
Canadian designer John Fluevog brings his colorful, funky style and distinctive brand of unique, comfortable, and trendy shoes for women as well as men to this historic quarter.

9 Hu's Shoes & Hu's Wear
MAP L3 ▪ 2906 M St, NW
Visit this chic boutique for high-end women's shoes and fashion from emerging designers that you won't find in department stores.

10 Georgetown Tobacco
MAP L3 ▪ 3144 M St, NW
A neighborhood fixture for more than 40 years, this quaint tobacco shop sells more than 100 brands of cigars, hand-sculpted pipes, and humidors.

Places to Eat

PRICE CATEGORIES
For a three-course meal for one with half a bottle of wine (or equivalent meal), taxes and extra charges.

$ under $50 $$ $50–100 $$$ over $100

1 Farmers Fishers Bakers
MAP L3 ▪ 3000 K St, NW ▪ 202-298-8783 ▪ $$

From the same folks that created the phenomenally popular Founding Farmers *(see p103)*, this Washington Harbour restaurant offers seasonal, agriculturally sustainable, farm-to-table cuisine, with something for everyone – juicy steaks, pizza, jambalaya, and ultra-fresh sushi and fish dishes.

2 1789
MAP K2 ▪ 1226 36th St, NW ▪ 202-965-1789 ▪ $$$

Serving excellent American food, this elegant townhouse *(see p69)* is divided into six themed rooms, and was popular with President Clinton.

3 Sequoia
MAP L3 ▪ 3000 K St, NW ▪ 202-944-4200 ▪ $$

Famous for its beautiful views of the Potomac River, this is a haven for people-watching. The modern American cuisine, emphasizing seafood, enhances the setting.

4 Das Ethiopian Cuisine
MAP L2 ▪ 1201 28th St, NW ▪ 202-333-4710 ▪ $

The large Ethiopian population in the city has produced a number of fine restaurants; this one is rated among the best. Delicious vegetarian dishes, as well as spicy meat and poultry.

5 Baked & Wired
MAP L3 ▪ 1052 Thomas Jefferson St, NW ▪ $

Well known for its baked goods and crafted coffee drinks, Baked & Wired is a popular community hot spot.

6 Cafe Milano
MAP L2 ▪ 3251 Prospect St, NW ▪ 202-333-6183 ▪ $$$

This charming Italian restaurant has been serving exquisite dishes since 1992.

7 El Centro D.F.
MAP L2 ▪ 1218 Wisconsin Ave, NW ▪ 202-333-4100 ▪ $

Savor soulful takes on traditional Mexican tacos and street food.

8 Martin's Tavern
MAP L2 ▪ 1264 Wisconsin Ave, NW ▪ 202-333-7370 ▪ $$

Good tavern fare, a great bar, and a legendary booth in which John F. Kennedy proposed to Jackie.

9 Fiola Mare
MAP L3 ▪ 3050 K St, NW ▪ 202-525-1402 ▪ $$$

With superb views over the Potomac, this restaurant offers impeccably pre-pared seafood and top-notch service.

10 Clyde's of Georgetown
MAP L3 ▪ 3236 M St, NW ▪ 202-333-9180 ▪ $$

This long-time Georgetown favorite incorporates seasonal and local produce into its special menu items.

The elegant Clyde's of Georgetown

See map on p104

⟦TOP 10⟧ Beyond the City Center

Mount Vernon greenhouse

Washington's monumental core is so rich in sights that visitors may be tempted to look no farther. But many delights lie within easy reach of the city center. The U Street NW corridor is a historic town center for the African American community; Bethesda is full of fine restaurants; the Southwest waterfront is busy with commercial fishing activity; while Old Town Alexandria has a beautifully restored downtown. In complete contrast, there's the wilder side of the stately Potomac River at Great Falls.

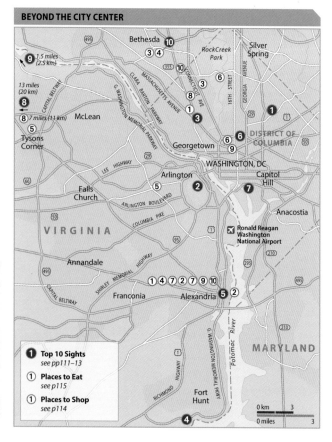

BEYOND THE CITY CENTER

1 Top 10 Sights
see pp111–13

1 Places to Eat
see p115

1 Places to Shop
see p114

Basilica of the National Shrine of the Immaculate Conception

1 Basilica of the National Shrine of the Immaculate Conception

MAP D3 ▪ 400 Michigan Ave, NE ▪ 202-526-8300 ▪ Open Apr–Oct: 7am–7pm daily; Nov–Mar: 7am–6pm daily ▪ www.nationalshrine.com

This mammoth basilica incorporates more than 60 chapels and oratories that retell the diverse history of the Roman Catholic Church in the United States. Conceived in the grand style, it is the largest Roman Catholic church in the Western hemisphere. The building combines Byzantine and Romanesque features, creating an intensely decorative but substantial effect. The interior is overwhelming in its grandeur. There is also an on-site cafeteria serving breakfast and lunch, which is convenient because there are few nearby restaurants. Free guided tours are available.

2 Arlington National Cemetery

A visit to this solemn burial ground (see pp34–5) brings conflicting emotions – pride in the defenders of freedom, pleasure in the presence of its great beauty, but dismay at the loss of countless lives marked by the arrays of headstones.

3 Washington National Cathedral

This noble church (see pp30–31), completed in 1990, is a triumph of the English Gothic style, handcrafted using authentic methods.

4 Mount Vernon

Without a doubt a fascinating window into George Washington and the agrarian plantation life (see pp36–9) that was important in leading to the revolutionary break with Britain.

5 Old Town Alexandria

MAP D5

This lovely old city center, across the Potomac, just beneath the capital, retains the charm and hospitality of its illustrious past while giving visitors all modern conveniences, including a metro station (King Street on the yellow and blue lines). Alexandria is noted for its historical and archeological museums, Gadsby's Tavern (see p48), the evocative system of Civil War forts and defenses at Fort Ward, and its captivating residential architecture, shops, and restaurants.

Townhouses in Old Town Alexandria

6 U Street, NW
MAP N1

For much of the 20th century, U Street, NW, was the main street of this prosperous African American neighborhood. Opened as a movie theater in 1922, the Lincoln Theatre (see p67) has now been refurbished and presents performances of every kind. Next door is the famous Ben's Chili Bowl, turning out great simple food for capacity crowds. The legendary jazz musician Duke Ellington (see p47) played his first paid performance at True Reformer Hall at the junction of 12th and U Street, NW. The poignant sculpture and plaza of the African American Civil War Memorial (see p51) commemorates African Americans who served their country in the Civil War.

7 National Zoo
MAP J4 ■ 3001 Connecticut Ave, NW ■ 202-633-4888 ■ Grounds: open mid-Mar–Sep: 8am–7pm (Oct–mid-Mar: to 5pm) ■ Buildings: open mid-Mar–Sep: 9am–6pm daily; (Oct–mid-Mar: to 4pm) ■ Closed Dec 25 ■ www.nationalzoo.si.edu

Home to around 300 species of animals, many of which are rare or endangered, this zoological park is considered to be one of the most environmentally friendly in the world. It was established by an act of Congress in 1889 and is a part of the Smithsonian Institution. Located northwest of the city center,

---

NATIONAL CATHEDRAL SCHOOLS

Like a medieval basilica, National Cathedral is surrounded by some of the most prestigious prep schools in the city. St. Albans' alumni include Al Gore and Jesse Jackson, Jr. The all-girls National Cathedral School is alma mater to a number of Rockefellers and Roosevelts. Sidwell Friends School, just along Wisconsin Avenue, educated Chelsea Clinton, the Nixon daughters, Nancy Davis Reagan, and Barack Obama's daughters.

---

in the Woodley Park neighborhood, the park covers an area of 163 acres (66 ha) and delights over two million visitors annually. The Education Center offers maps at the entrance where you can check for feeding times. Guided tours directed by animal experts are available.

8 National Air and Space Museum Steven F. Udvar-Hazy Center

This display and restoration center for some of the museum's magnificent collection of historic aviation and space artifacts (see pp20–21) opened in December 2003 near Dulles International Airport. Two giant hangars with accompanying support buildings, sprawled across 17 acres (7 ha), feature thousands of artifacts, including the space shuttle *Discovery*, a Concorde, and a Lockheed SR-71 Blackbird.

National Air and Space Museum Steven F. Udvar-Hazy Center

⑨ Great Falls

MAP A2 ■ Falls: open dawn–dusk daily ■ Great Falls Park Visitor Center: 9200 Old Dominion Dr, McLean, VA; 703-757-3101; www.nps.gov/grfa

About 15 miles (24 km) north of Washington, DC, the Potomac is rent by magnificent waterfalls over the crags and sluices of the eroded river bed. In the state of Virginia, Great Falls Park is reached from Old Dominion Drive (Route 738). It overlooks the river, hiking trails, and the ruins of a small 19th-century town. On the Maryland side, the Great Falls area is part of the C&O Canal (see p105). The Great Falls Park Visitor Center has trail maps and a short video about the park. There are remarkable river views from the overlook on Olmstead Island.

Whitewater rapids at Great Falls

⑩ Bethesda, Maryland

MAP C2

Locally, Bethesda is best known for its enormous quantity and range of restaurants, most of them clustered into a lively downtown area that still retains the charming atmosphere of a traditional town center. The high-end professional employment offered by Bethesda's world-renowned biotechnology industry has also generated a spirited music, performance, and arts scene that caters to its cultured and wealthy residents. The city is especially strong on public art. Its streets and parks spotlight distinguished contemporary works in every style, by way of sculpture and stunning painted murals.

A DAY IN OLD TOWN ALEXANDRIA

▶ MORNING

Begin at **Christ Church** (118 N Washington St; open 9am–4pm Mon–Sat, 2–4pm Sun; donation), a handsome Georgian-style building completed in 1773. George Washington's box pew has been preserved. Then turn right onto Cameron Street toward the harbor. Continue three blocks and turn right onto North Royal Street. The two buildings on your right comprise **Gadsby's Tavern Museum** (see p48). The tours involve an introduction to colonial life in the city. Continue one block and turn left onto King Street. On Saturday morning, the square hosts a historic Farmers Market. Continue south to the **Stabler-Leadbeater Apothecary Museum** (107 S Fairfax St; open Apr–Oct: 10am–5pm Tue–Sat, 1–5pm Mon & Sun; Nov–Mar: 11am–4pm Wed–Sat, 1pm–4pm Sun; adm). Here you will find herbal botanicals, handblown glass, and medical equipment from the 1800s.

AFTERNOON

 Enjoy lunch or a snack at one of the restaurants along King Street, then continue toward the harbor to North Union Street, and turn left to shop for original artwork at the popular **Torpedo Factory Art Center** (see p114), home to more than 80 working artist studios, plus nine galleries and the Bread & Water Company, which serves light fare. Directly behind the art center is the **Potomac Riverboat Company** (potomacriverboatco.com), which runs water taxis to the National Harbor, District Wharf, and Georgetown.

See map on p110 ⬅

Places to Shop

Shoppers at the National Harbor

1 National Harbor
MAP D6 ■ 165 Waterfront St, National Harbor, MD 20745

Seventy shops line the streets of this trendy neighborhood. Designer jewelry and fashion are prominent, as are specialty shops selling fine foods, wines, and even motorcycles. Nearby Tanger offers another 80 plus brand-name outlets.

2 The Shoe Hive
MAP D5 ■ 127 S Fairfax St, Alexandria, VA ■ www.theshoe hive.com

Opened in 2003, this local boutique has proved itself to be a superb predictor of fashion trends. It specializes in stylish brands such as Golden Goose, Paul Green, Mou Mou, and Veja.

3 Politics and Prose
MAP H2 ■ 5015 Connecticut Ave, NW

A bookstore with a large selection of works on politics, culture, and government. A cheerful place, despite its serious stock, with a café.

4 Fibre Space
MAP C5 ■ 1319 Prince St, Alexandria, VA 22314

This Old Town Alexandria shop is filled with a dazzling assortment of colorful yarns from local, sustainable sources. Knitting equipment such as needles, crochet hooks, patterns, and more can be found here.

5 Tysons Corner Center and Tysons Galleria
1961 Chain bridge Rd, McLean, VA & 2001 International Drive, McLean, VA

This huge shopping site has stores as well as cinemas and restaurants.

6 Kramerbooks
MAP N2 ■ 1517 Connecticut Ave, NW

This Dupont Circle landmark has a fantastic collection of books and knowledgeable staff. There's also a bar and restaurant, the Afterwords Café. The store is open until 3am on Fridays and Saturdays.

7 Torpedo Factory Art Center
MAP D5 ■ 105 N Union St, Alexandria, VA

Originally a torpedo-making factory, today the site contains 82 studios and nine galleries where artists and craftspeople create artworks and offer it for sale. Find prints, ceramics, photography, painting, and sculptures.

8 Tempo Bookstore
MAP G3 ■ 4115 Wisconsin Ave, NW 105 ■ www.tempobookstore.com

Browse books on English and foreign languages at this shop. It also has a great selection for kids.

9 Chocolate Moose
MAP N3 ■ 1743 L St NW ■ 202-463-0992

This shop specializes in the weird and wonderful. You will find confections, housewares, toys and much more.

10 The Collection at Chevy Chase
MAP G2 ■ 5471 Wisconsin Ave, Chevy Chase, MD ■ www.collectionchevy chase.com

A high-end mall with stores such as Saks Fifth Avenue and Tiffany & Co., and a wide range of restaurants.

Places to Eat

PRICE CATEGORIES
For a three-course meal for one with half a bottle of wine (or equivalent meal), taxes and extra charges.
....
$ under $50 $$ $50–100 $$$ over $100

1 2amys
MAP H4 ▪ 3715 Macomb St, NW ▪ 202-885-5700 ▪ $

Within easy walking distance of the National Cathedral, this is the favorite pizzeria of the locals. Expect to wait for a table during peak times. Authentic Neapolitan pizzas baked in a wood-burning oven.

2 Vermilion
MAP C5 ▪ 1120 King St, Alexandria, VA 22314 ▪ 703-684-9669 ▪ $$

Consistently listed among the best restaurants in Alexandria, Vermilion (see p68) serves New American cuisine featuring farm-to-table ingredients in lively versions of traditional favorites.

3 Bacchus of Lebanon
MAP C2 ▪ 7945 Norfolk Ave, Bethesda, MD ▪ 301-657-1722 ▪ $$

Don't miss the delicious meze at this Lebanese restaurant. Marinated chicken, roast eggplant (aubergine), hummus, and squid fill numerous little dishes with flavor.

4 Passage to India
MAP C2 ▪ 4931 Cordell Ave, Bethesda, MD ▪ 301-656-3373 ▪ $$

The menu here does not limit itself to any particular region of India. The dal (lentils) and butter chicken are rich and smooth – a must-have.

5 Grand Cru
MAP B4 ▪ 4301 Wilson Blvd, Arlington, VA ▪ 703-243-7900 ▪ $$

This tiny café has an exquisite menu, including succulent filet mignon and rich crème brûlée. Doubling as a wine shop, it has a great selection available. Dine in the courtyard in good weather.

6 Fat Pete's BBQ
MAP H4 ▪ 3407 Connecticut Ave, NW ▪ 202-362-7777 ▪ $

With preparation styles that run the gamut from Texas to the Carolinas, meat dishes abound at Fat Pete's BBQ.

7 The Wharf
MAP D5 ▪ 119 King St, Alexandria, VA ▪ 703-836-2836 ▪ $$

Housed in a historic building that features 1790s style architecture, this restaurant offers excellent seafood.

8 Ted's Bulletin
11948 Market St, Reston, VA 20190 ▪ 703-956-9510 ▪ $

A modern version of the traditional American diner, this spot offers an inviting atmosphere, a large selection of beers, and a classic grill menu. It is open for brunch, lunch, and dinner.

Delicious steak at Ted's Bulletin

9 Le Refuge
MAP C5 ▪ 127 N Washington St, Alexandria, VA ▪ 703-548-4661 ▪ $$$

This cozy wood-beamed French bistro remains a local favorite. The escargot and the mustard-sauced rack of lamb are highly recommended.

10 Taverna Cretekou
MAP D5 ▪ 818 King St, Alexandria, VA ▪ 703-548-8688 ▪ $

Fantastic Greek food, ouzo, and traditional dancing can be found at this popular restaurant.

See map on p110

Streetsmart

U Street/African-Amer Civil War
Memorial/Cardozo metro station

Getting Around	118
Practical Information	122
Places to Stay	126
General Index	134
Acknowledgments	142
Street Index	144

Getting Around

Arriving by Air

Washington, DC is served by three major airports. International flights arrive at **Dulles International Airport (IAD)**, internal flights arrive at **Reagan National Airport (DCA)**, and low-cost international and internal flights fly into **Baltimore/Washington International Thurgood Marshall Airport (BWI)**.

The **Washington Flyer** Silver Line Express Bus connects Dulles to Wiehle-Reston East Metrorail station, which has services into DC. Alternatively, Metrobus Route 5A runs to central DC, or you can take a cab or Uber.

From BWI, **Maryland Rail Commuter Service (MARC)** and Amtrak offer train services into DC. Trains run between BWI and DC's Union Station on a regular basis. Taxis and Ubers are also available.

Reagan National is served by the Metrorail (blue and yellow lines), with travel time to and from downtown typically around 20 minutes. Both Uber and taxi services are available, too.

Domestic Train Travel

Traveling by train is one of the best ways to reach the DC area. **Amtrak**, the national train operator of the US, runs direct trains between Washington, DC and major cities, such as Baltimore, Philadelphia, and Williamsburg. All trains arrive at the large Union Station, located near the Capitol. The station is easily accessible by Metrorail and Metrobus.

Amtrak offers a deluxe train service to New York City, called the Acela, which is faster and more comfortable than the regular train, but is more expensive. Both Acela and the slower Northeast Regional trains to New York leave every hour. Maryland's regional commuter train, MARC, has regular fast services to Baltimore.

If traveling widely across the country, it may be worth buying a USA Rail Pass, which gives reduced fares, and can be bought on the Amtrak website.

Long-Distance Bus Travel

Intercity buses are an excellent, economical way to get to Washington, DC. As well as the traditional Greyhound buses, there are half a dozen bus companies serving DC, including **Megabus**, the **Washington Deluxe**, and **FlixBus**. Many of these buses are equipped with restrooms and free Wi-Fi.

Tickets are sold on a scale – a one-way ticket to New York generally costs about $30, but may end up costing as little as $1 with advance purchase, which is always cheaper than buying on the day.

Greyhound buses depart from the bus terminal near Union Station, but many of the other bus companies leave from more central locations throughout the city.

Public Transportation

Washington Metropolitan Area Transit Authority (**WMATA**) is Washington, DC's main public transportation provider. Safety and hygiene measures, timetables, ticket information, transport maps, and more can be obtained from the WMATA website.

Tickets

Metrorail has phased out paper tickets in favor of SmarTrip cards and device contactless payments. Rechargeable SmarTrip cards can be used not only on Metrorail services but also on city buses and other regional transit systems. On buses you can also pay with cash: place your exact fare in coins or dollar bills in the fare box near the driver (the driver does not carry cash to make change).

SmarTrip cards can be bought and topped up online, from Metrorail vending machines at stations, or from Metro retail outlets. A SmarTrip card costs $2 and can be loaded with cash on a pay as you go basis or various passes, including for one day ($13), three days ($28), and seven days ($58). The cost of individual fares depends on the time and distance you wish to travel; the base fare starts from $2 off-peak and $2.25 at peak times. It is more expensive to travel during rush hour. You can also pay for travel through Apple Pay or Google Pay on your smartphone.

Metrorail

For most destinations in the city, Metrorail, the subway-surface rail system, is the best way to get around. Metrorail consists of six color-coded lines: Red, Blue, Orange, Yellow, Green, and Silver. Trains run from 5am to 11:30pm Monday through Thursday, from 5am to 1am on Friday, from 7am to 1am on Saturday, and from 8am to 11pm on Sunday. Trains run frequently (every 10 minutes or less) and stops are announced at every station. Peak times (5–9:30am and 3–7pm Monday–Friday) are best avoided.

Each Metro station works on three levels: street level, where you enter; mezzanine, where ticket machines are located; and the platform, which is accessed by escalator or elevator. Use the Metro map to figure out which line you need for your destination and the terminus you will be heading for. The terminus denotes the direction the train is traveling and will be on signs in the station, guiding you to the correct platform. Where there is more than one line, follow the signs first for the line that you want and then the platform.

Tap your SmarTrip card or scan your mobile device on the reader at the rail station fare gate when entering and leaving.

The WMATA website has regular updates on travel disruptions and closures due to track maintenance.

MetroBus

MetroBus is a fast, inexpensive way to get around Washington, DC and connect to numerous outlying districts.

Fares can be paid either with exact change when you board the bus or with a SmarTrip card, which can be purchased online. Transfers are free within a three-hour period for SmarTrip card users. All other tickets are non-transferable; if changing buses after paying with exact change you will need to pay for a new fare. Up to two children under the age of five can travel for free with a fare-paying passenger, and there are discounts available for travelers with disabilities and senior citizens.

Bus stops are identified by red, white, and blue signs. Signs list details of routes taken by all buses that use that stop. The bus will display both the route number and its terminus. Buses do not stop automatically; you will need to flag one down at a designated stop if you wish to board. Stops are announced on board. Pull on the line running along the top of the windows to request a stop. Always exit the bus at the back.

The **DC Circulator** bus (see p106) is popular with visitors. It links most of Washington, DC's main sights and attractions, and runs every 10 minutes. Fares are $1 for adults and 50 cents for children (under-5s travel free with a paying adult). Maps of all the bus routes are available in Metrorail stations, and maps of specific lines are posted at each bus stop.

DIRECTORY

ARRIVING BY AIR

Baltimore/Washington International Thurgood Marshall Airport (BWI)
ⓦ bwiairport.com

Dulles International Airport (IAD)
ⓦ flydulles.com

Maryland Rail Commuter Service (MARC)
ⓦ mta.maryland.gov

Reagan National Airport (DCA)
ⓦ flyreagan.com

Washington Flyer
ⓦ flydulles.com/iad/silver-line-express-bus-metrorail-station

DOMESTIC TRAIN TRAVEL

Amtrak
ⓦ amtrak.com

LONG-DISTANCE BUS TRAVEL

FlixBus
ⓦ flixbus.com

Greyhound
ⓦ greyhound.com

Megabus
ⓦ megabus.com

Washington Deluxe
ⓦ washny.com

PUBLIC TRANSPORTATION

WMATA
ⓦ wmata.com

METROBUS

DC Circulator
ⓦ dccirculator.com

Bus Tours

Several companies offer bus tours of Washington, DC's historic surroundings. **Gray Line** takes you on the Black Heritage tour, to Gettysburg National Military Park, Colonial Williamsburg, or Jefferson's home, Monticello. Several companies offer open-top tours. Passengers can hop on and off at any stop, and one- or two-day passes are available. **City Sights DC** organizes combination day trips covering Washington, DC's most popular landmarks, monuments, and points of interest. **USA Guided Tours**, meanwhile, offers smaller luxury bus tours, including night tours of the city and a tour dedicated to African American history and culture in Washington, DC. Private tours are also available.

Taxis

There are designated taxi ranks across the city. The **Department of For-Hire Vehicles** has an interactive map of taxi stands in the district. In addition, taxis wait near major sights, offices, and hotels. It is less easy to hail a taxi on the street. **DC Yellow Cab** is a reliable taxi company that can be pre-booked.

Taxi fares in DC are operated using time and distance meters. Passengers should expect to pay a starting "drop" rate of $3.50, and then $2.16 for every mile after this. Luggage, extra pick-ups, and rush hour travel can all incur surcharges.

Taxis charge $25.00 per hour for waiting. Be aware that drivers do not always know the way to addresses beyond the tourist center. Taxi app companies such as **Uber** and **Lyft** also operate in the city.

Driving

There is much to see beyond Washington's city limits, and traveling by car is easy with a GPS. However, driving is not the most efficient way to get around in the core DC area. Traffic congestion, one-way streets, and time-of-day parking restrictions can make driving difficult . Avoid rush hour (5–9:30am and 3–7pm Monday–Saturday), when there is not only a high volume of traffic but rush-hour tolls are imposed on some roads.

Washington, DC's road network forms a grid. Most numbered streets run north and south, and most lettered streets east and west. Diagonal streets running at a 45-degree angle criss-cross the grid in both directions and have a full road name, which is usually the name of a state.

Addresses contain NE, SE, SW, or NW, indicating their position relative to the Capitol building, which is at the center of the grid. Every address in DC includes the quadrant code, and its use is necessary to distinguish the precise location you are trying to reach.

Be aware that there is no "J," "X," "Y," or "Z" Street, and "I" Street is written as "Eye" Street.

Car Rental

Rental car companies are located at airports, Union Station, and many other locations. To rent a car in the US you must be at least 25 years old and have a valid driver's license and a clean record. All agencies require a major credit card.

Rental rates can vary wildly depending on the season, but no matter what time of year you're visiting, it's always cheaper to book in advance.

Getting damage and liability insurance is highly recommended. It is advisable to return the car with a full tank of gas, otherwise you will be required to pay the inflated fuel prices charged by the car rental agencies. Before you set off, check for any pre-existing damage to the car and make sure you note this on your contract.

Parking

Parking in a lot will cost you about $30 per day or about $12 for two hours. Street parking meters have a two-hour maximum stay, and fines are high.

Parking is prohibited on many downtown streets during rush hour. You can find specific time restrictions signposted on curbside signs. Your car will be towed if you disregard them.

Gasoline (Petrol)

There are over a hundred gas stations in the city. Gas comes in three grades – regular, mid-range, and premium. Most stations are exclusively self-service and only accept credit cards.

Rules of the Road

All drivers are required to carry a valid driver's license and must be able to produce registration documents and insurance for their vehicle. Most foreign licenses are valid, but if your license is not in English, or does not have a photo ID, you must get an International Driving Permit (IDP) in advance of your trip.

Traffic drives on the right-hand side of the road. Seat belts are compulsory in front seats and suggested in the back; children under three must ride in a child seat in the back. Belts are also compulsory in cabs.

You can turn right at a red light as long as you first come to a complete stop, and if there are no signs that prohibit it. A flashing yellow light at an intersection means slow down, look for oncoming traffic, and proceed with caution. Passing (overtaking) is allowed on any multilane road, and you must pass on the left. On smaller roads safe passing places are shown by a broken yellow line on your side of the double-yellow line. Crossing a double-yellow line, either by U-turn or by passing the car in front, is illegal, and will incur a fine if caught.

If a school bus stops to let passengers off, all traffic from both sides must stop and wait for the bus to drive off.

A limit of 0.08 percent blood alcohol is strictly enforced. For drivers under the age of 21 there is a zero-tolerance policy for drunk-driving. Driving while intoxicated (DWI) is a punishable offense that incurs heavy fines or even a prison sentence. Do not drink if you plan to drive.

In the event of an accident or breakdown, drivers of rental cars should contact their car rental company first. Members of the American Automobile Association (**AAA**) can have their vehicle towed to the nearest service station for repairs.

Cycling

There is a handy network of cycle routes throughout the city, with some main roads offering dedicated cycle lanes.

Capital Bikeshare has bicycles for rent at around 500 locations. One-day, three-day, or monthly passes are available. **Bike and Roll** offers bike rentals, as well as organized tours of the city. Rentals can be made by phone or instore from a minimum of two hours ($16) to a maximum of one day ($40). They provide helmets, some equipment such as locks, bicycle pumps, and puncture repair kits, as well as bicycle route maps of the city.

Some cycle lanes are also used by buses and taxis. Bicycles can be taken on buses, but must be stowed on racks at the front.

Walking

Washington is a city built for walking, with numerous green spaces, wide sidewalks, and courteous drivers. Busy streets have pedestrian walk lights at intersections.

While many of the main sights and monuments are clustered around the Mall, other attractions are quite spread out, so be sure to pack a pair of comfortable shoes.

Allow around two hours to cover the main sights of the city from the Washington Monument to the Lincoln Memorial and around the Tidal Basin. If you get tired of walking, you can hop on the DC Circulator (see p119) to see the sights from a city bus. Be aware, however, that traffic in Washington, DC can often be slow moving.

DIRECTORY

BUS TOURS

City Sights DC
Ⓦ citysightsdc.com

Gray Line
Ⓦ graylinedc.com

USA Guided Tours
Ⓦ usaguidedtours.com

TAXIS

DC Yellow Cab
Ⓦ dcyellowcab.com

Department of For-Hire Vehicles
Ⓦ dfhv.dc.gov

Lyft
Ⓦ lyft.com

Uber
Ⓦ uber.com

RULES OF THE ROAD

AAA
Ⓦ aaa.com

CYCLING

Bike and Roll
Ⓦ bikeandrolldc.com

Capital Bikeshare
Ⓦ capitalbikeshare.com

Practical Information

Passports and Visas

For entry requirements, including visas, consult your nearest US embassy or check the website of the **US Department of State**.

Canadian visitors require valid passports to enter the US. Citizens of 39 countries, including Australia, New Zealand, the UK, and the EU do not need a visa, but must have a passport and apply to enter in advance via the **Electronic System for Travel Authorization (ESTA)**. All other visitors require a tourist visa and passport to enter the US.

Government Advice

Now more than ever, it is important to consult both your and the US government's advice before travelling. The **UK Foreign and Commonwealth Office**, the US Department of State (see above), and the **Australian Department of Foreign Affairs and Trade** offer the latest information on security, health and local regulations.

Customs Information

You can find information on the laws relating to goods and currency taken in or out of the US on the **US Customs and Border Protection Agency** website.

Insurance

We recommend that you take out a comprehensive insurance policy covering theft, loss of belongings, medical care, cancellations and delays, and read the small print carefully.

Insurance is particularly important when travelling to Washington, DC as there is no universal healthcare in the US for citizens or visitors and so the cost of medical care is high. If coming from abroad, check with your primary healthcare insurer at home to see if you have any coverage while in the US.

Health

The US has a world-class healthcare system. Payment of medical expenses is the patient's responsibility. It is therefore important to arrange comprehensive medical insurance before traveling.

No specific inoculations are required to visit the US. For information regarding COVID-19 vaccination requirements, consult government advice.

Unless otherwise stated, tap water in Washington, DC is safe to drink.

Pack medications in their original, labeled containers. You can carry unused syringes and injectable prescription medication. Your hotel will usually recommend a doctor if you need one.

MedStar Georgetown University Hospital has a free weekday physician referral service, while **Children's National** is one of the country's top pediatric centers. Walk-in clinics such as **Farragut Medical and Travel Care** are also available, and for minor injuries some pharmacies have nurse practitioners. Pharmacies are an excellent source of advice. They can diagnose minor ailments and suggest appropriate treatment. Some pharmacies have walk-in clinics attached to treat common illnesses and minor injuries. One such clinic is the **CVS Minute Clinic**, which has nine locations in DC. For immediate treatment in an emergency, call 911 for an ambulance. For emergency dental care, contact **1-800-dentist**.

Smoking, Alcohol, and Drugs

Smoking is prohibited in all enclosed public spaces. Cigarettes can be purchased by those over 18 years old; proof of age is required.

The legal minimum age for drinking alcohol in Washington is 21, and you will need photo ID as proof of age. It is illegal to drink alcohol in public parks or to carry an open container of alcohol in your car, and penalties for driving under the influence of alcohol are severe (p197).

Possession of illegal drugs is prohibited and could result in a prison sentence.

ID

It is not compulsory to carry ID at all times in Washington, DC. If you are asked by police to show your ID, a photocopy of your passport (and visa if applicable) should suffice.

Personal Security

Washington, DC is generally safe and visits are nearly always trouble-free. As in many large cities, petty crime does exist, however, so be alert to your surroundings. Be wary of pickpockets on public transportation and in crowded tourist areas.

If you have anything stolen, report the crime within 24 hours to the nearest police station and take ID with you. If you need to make an insurance claim, get a copy of the crime report. Contact your embassy if you have your passport stolen, or in the event of a serious crime or accident.

As a rule, residents of Washington, DC are very accepting of all people regardless of their race, gender, or sexuality. DC is a diverse, multicultural city, with a significant African American heritage, one of the largest LGBTQ+ populations in the US, and a strong history of minority activism. Same-sex marriages were legalized in 2009, and in 2013 the district recognized the rights of those wanting to legally change their gender. Destination DC, the city's tourist website (see below), lists LGBTQ+ events and festivals, bars, and clubs.

For ambulance, medical, police, and fire brigade services, call the national **emergency services** number 911 and provide both your location and details about the problem.

Travelers with Specific Requirements

Washington, DC is one of the most accessible cities in the US, but there are challenges involved with some historic buildings, restaurants, and shops. Government buildings, museums and theaters are generally accessible, but always call ahead to ensure that any specific requirements will be met.

Metrorail stations and trains are accessible, featuring extra-wide gates and elevators. Rail cars have gap reducers, priority seating, and emergency intercoms that also include instructions in Braille and raised alphabet. All Metrobuses are wheelchair friendly and have lifts or ramps for easy access Visitors can find more information about public transportation accessibility on the **Metro** website.

Mobility Works rents wheelchair-friendly vehicles in various locations throughout the are, while **ScootAround** offers wheelchair and scooter rentals.

Destination DC provides detailed information, tips, and general assistance for visitors with specific requirements. **Columbia Lighthouse For the Blind** is a useful resource for visually impaired travelers, while the Jeenie app includes on-demand American Sign Language interpreting via video-chat.

DIRECTORY

PASSPORTS AND VISAS

Electronic System for Travel Authorization (ESTA)
🌐 esta.cbp.dhs.gov/esta

US Department of State
🌐 travel.state.gov

GOVERNMENT ADVICE

Australian Department of Foreign Affairs and Trade
🌐 smartraveller.gov.au

UK Foreign and Commonwealth Office
🌐 gov.uk/foreign-travel-advice

CUSTOMS INFORMATION

US Customs and Border Protection Agency
🌐 cbp.gov/travel

HEALTH

1-800-dentist
🌐 1800dentist.com

Children's National
🌐 childrensnational.org

CVS Minute Clinic
🌐 cvs.com/minuteclinic

Farragut Medical and Travel Care
🌐 farragutmedical.com

MedStar Georgetown University Hospital
🌐 medstargeorgetown.org

PERSONAL SECURITY

Emergency Services
📞 911

TRAVELERS WITH SPECIFIC REQUIREMENTS

Columbia Lighthouse For the Blind
🌐 clb.org

Destination DC
🌐 washington.org

Metro
🌐 wmata.com/accessibility/

Mobility Works
🌐 mobilityworks.com

ScootAround
🌐 scootaround.com

Time Zone

Washington, DC is on Eastern Standard Time (EST), and is three hours ahead of California and five hours behind London. Daylight Saving Time starts at 2am on the second Sunday in March and ends at 2am on the first Sunday in November.

Money

The US currency is the dollar ($). Most establishments accept major credit, debit, and prepaid currency cards. Contactless payments are becoming increasingly common, but cash is usually required by smaller shops and businesses, and by street vendors. DC's Metro services rolled out contactless payment options in 2020.

Tipping is customary. In restaurants it is normal to tip 20 percent of the total bill and $1 per drink in a bar. Allow for a tip of 15 percent for taxi drivers. Hotel porters and housekeeping expect $3–$5 per bag or day.

Electrical Appliances

The standard US electric current is 110 volts and 60 Hz current. American plugs have two flat pins; an adapter will be needed for European appliances.

Mobile Phones and Wi-Fi

Cell phone service in Washington is excellent. If you're coming from overseas and want to guarantee that your cell phone will work, make sure you have a quad-band phone.

Check with your service provider before you travel; you may also need to activate the "roaming" facility. Other options include buying a prepaid cell phone in the US or a SIM chip for a US carrier.

Free Wi-Fi hotspots can be found throughout the city in public libraries, parks, and throughout the Golden Triangle area. Visit the **Washington DC Free Wi-Fi Access** website to find the nearest free Wi-Fi spot near you. Free Wi-Fi is also available in all underground Metrorail stations. Cafés and restaurants will usually permit the use of their Wi-Fi on the condition that you make a purchase and some hotels offer free Wi-Fi to guests.

Mail

US Postal Service (USPS) runs the postal system in the US. Stamps can be purchased from most major supermarkets and in post offices – most are open from 9am to 5pm Monday to Friday, with a limited Saturday service, usually 9am to noon. Blue mailboxes are for letters only. Small packages must be taken to a post office. Depending on how far the mail needs to travel in the US, it can take from one to five days to arrive at its destination.

Weather

The average DC daytime temperature ranges from a high of 89° F (32° C) in July to a low of 42° F (6° C) in January; the average nighttime temperature goes from a high of 72° F (22° C) in July to a low of

26° F (-3° C) in January. However, temperatures in every season vary greatly. Humidity can be an issue in summer. Precipitation averages range from a high of 4 in (10 cm) in August to a low of 3 in (7 cm) in January when much of it falls as snow. Winters can be raw, with snow and ice storms that can paralyze the city.

Opening Hours

Office hours are usually 9am to 5pm. Stores open at 9 or 10am and close around 5 or 6pm Monday to Saturday. Some stores remain open later, and Sunday store hours vary. Grocery stores generally open 8am to 9pm daily, or longer. Some larger stores are open 24 hours. Pharmacy hours vary, from 8am to 6pm or later, and some have 24-hour service. Most banks are open 9am to 5pm Monday to Friday, and some also open Saturday morning. Most museums are open from 10am to 5:30pm, but check as times and dates can vary. Metrorail trains start at 5am Monday to Friday, 7am Saturday, and 8am on Sunday, and stop at 11:30pm from Monday to Thursday, 1am Friday and Saturday, and 11pm Sunday. Public holiday hours may be different, so check ahead of time.

COVID-19 Increased rates of infection may result in temporary opening hours and/or closures. Always check ahead before visiting museums, attractions and hospitality venues.

Visitor Information

Destination DC *(see p123)*, Washington's official tourism site, provides information on the city's history, attractions, dining, accommodation, tours, and events, and offers useful interactive maps. Assistance is also available by phone and at their office on 7th Street, NW. The **Capitol Visitor Center** and the nonprofit **Cultural Tourism DC** are also excellent sources of visitor information.

The **DC Eater** website has excellent information on the latest restaurant news and food events, while the comprehensive **DCist** website is a local favorite for city news, events, and openings.

The **Smithsonian Mobile** is a handy digital guide to the Smithsonian featuring information on opening hours, floor plans, and special events.

Washington, DC offers a number of visitor passes and discount cards (available to buy online and from participating tourist offices) for exhibitions, events, museum entry, and even transportation. These include the **Go Washington DC Pass** and the **Washington DC Sightseeing Pass**. Entry to all Smithsonian sites is free.

Local Customs

Be respectful when visiting national monuments and sights of national significance.

You can be fined for littering. Dispose of your waste in garbage cans. Use the blue bins on the National Mall and in most museums to recycle bottles and cans.

Ensure that you are dressed modestly when visiting religious buildings; cover your torso and upper arms; ensure shorts and skirts cover your knees.

Language

While the main language spoken in Washington, DC is English, followed closely by Spanish, this is a cosmopolitan city in which you will hear multiple languages. Many attractions and tour companies cater to those with limited English by offering foreign-language headsets, museum guides, and information packs.

Taxes and Refunds

Taxes will be added to hotel and restaurant charges, theater tickets, some grocery and store sales, and most other purchases. Always check if tax is included in the price displayed. Sales tax is 6 percent, hotel tax is 14.95 percent, and there is a 10 percent tax on food and beverages.

When tipping in a restaurant, it is the norm to include the tax in your calculation. A quick way to calculate restaurant tips is simply to double the tax, which adds up to about 18 percent.

Accommodations

Washington, DC offers a very wide range of accommodations options. High-rise hotels, historic inns, all-suites accommodations, and trendy boutique hotels can be found near the main attractions and Metro stations. Bed-and-breakfasts, apartments, and campgrounds are usually located farther from the city center.

Prices are lowest from January to early March. Spring and summer are popular and generally expensive, although weekend rates may be lower when Congress is not in session. Make sure to book well in advance to secure the best deals. Rates are subject to an additional 14.95 percent room tax.

A comprehensive list of accommodations to suit all needs can be found on Destination DC, the city's official tourism website *(see p123)*.

DIRECTORY

MOBILE PHONES AND WI-FI

Washington DC Free Wi-Fi Access
w octo.dc.gov/wifi

MAIL

US Postal Service
w usps.com

VISITOR INFORMATION

Capitol Visitor Center
w visitthecapitol.gov

Cultural Tourism DC
w culturaltourismdc.org

DC Eater
w dc.easter.com

DCist
w dcist.com

Go Washington DC Pass
w gocity.com/washington-dc/en-us

Smithsonian Mobile
w si.edu/mobile

Washington DC Sightseeing Pass
w sightseeingpass.com/en/washington-dc

Places to Stay

PRICE CATEGORIES

For a standard, double room per night (with breakfast if included), taxes and extra charges.

$ under $200 $$ $200–350 $$$ over $350

Luxury Hotels

The Ritz-Carlton
MAP M3 ■ 1150 22nd St, NW ■ 202-835-0500 ■ www.ritzcarlton.com ■ $$

The Ritz-Carlton provides the finest quality furnishings, including Egyptian cotton sheets and down feather comforters. The marble bathrooms are spacious and luxurious. Pool and spa facilities are available on site.

Conrad Washington DC
MAP P3 ■ 950 New York Ave, NW ■ 202-844-5900 ■ www.hilton.com ■ $$$

One of the better luxury options in the heart of the city, the Conrad features large rooms, huge beds, floor-to-ceiling windows, premium cable TV, and espresso machines. It's also home to Estuary, a stylish restaurant from celebrity chefs Bryan and Michael Voltaggio.

Fairmont Washington DC
MAP M3 ■ 2401 M St, NW ■ 202-429-2400 ■ www.fairmont.com/washington ■ $$$

The garden courtyard at this luxury establishment is absolutely gorgeous, and there's a gym area and a great pool for guests to use. Only some of the Fairmont's rooms include balconies.

Four Seasons Hotel
MAP L3 ■ 2800 Pennsylvania Ave, NW ■ 202-342-0444 ■ www.fourseasons.com/washington ■ $$$

This is one of DC's best five-star hotels. The spa is renowned, and the hotel's Bourbon Steak restaurant is one of the best in the city. It's close to Georgetown and Rock Creek Park.

Gaylord National Resort and Convention Center
MAP D6 ■ 201 Waterfront St, National Harbor, MD ■ 301-965-4000 ■ www.marriott.com ■ $$$

The Gaylord National is the largest combined hotel and convention center on the East Coast. The 18-story glass atrium offers great views of the Potomac River and Alexandria.

The Graham Hotel
MAP L3 ■ 1075 Thomas Jefferson St, NW ■ 202-337-0900 ■ www.thegrahamgeorgetown.com ■ $$$

The Graham offers its guests every luxury in the heart of Georgetown, with spacious, tranquil suites and a roof-deck bar.

Grand Hyatt Washington
MAP Q3 ■ 1000 H St, NW ■ 202-582-1234 ■ www.hyatt.com ■ $$$

The atrium of the Grand Hyatt is airy and spacious with an adjacent Starbucks Reserve and the inviting Cure Bar & Bistro.

Mandarin Oriental Washington, DC
MAP P5 ■ 1330 Maryland Ave, SW ■ 202-554-8588 ■ www.mandarinoriental.com ■ $$$

Monumental views over the Potomac Tidal Basin and Jefferson Memorial (see p88) are to be had at this elegant hotel. Rooms boast king size beds and silk tapestries. There's also a spa and pool.

Park Hyatt Washington
MAP M2 ■ 1201 24th St, NW ■ 202-789-1234 ■ www.hyatt.com ■ $$$

The decor at this hotel features original moden artwork enhancing its elegant ambience. Park Hyatt Washington has an skylit indoor pool and a fitness center.

Riggs Washington DC
MAP P4 ■ 900 F St, NW ■ 202-788-2800 ■ www.riggsdc.com ■ $$$

Housed inside the elegant former premises of Riggs National Bank, this hotel has beautiful rooms designed by New York-based design studio Voutsa, with ornate wallpaper, marble bathrooms, and wood flooring.

Rosewood Washington DC
MAP L2 ■ 1050 31st St, NW ■ 202-617-2400 ■ www.rosewoodhotels.com ■ $$$

Located along the C&O Canal in the heart of historic Georgetown, this hotel offers a blend of old-world elegance and modern interiors.

Sofitel Lafayette Square

MAP P3 ■ 806 15th St, NW ■ 202-730-8800 ■ www. sofitel-washington-dc. com ■ $$$

On a corner of Lafayette Square, this 1862 building, transformed by the French Sofitel chain into an elegant hotel, has a gentleman's club-like ambience. The sound-proofing and acoustic doors are a welcome feature. The restaurant serves contemporary French bistro cuisine.

W Washington, DC

MAP P4 ■ 515 15th St, NW ■ 202-661-2400 ■ www. marriott.com ■ $$$

The city's historic Hotel Washington is now the W, a prestigious brand of Starwood Resorts and Hotels. Many of its luxury rooms have superb views of the White House and other major landmarks.

Historic Hotels

Hamilton Hotel

MAP P3 ■ 1001 14th St, NW ■ 202-682-0111 ■ www.hamiltonhoteldc. com ■ $

Open since 1922, this distinguished hotel offers elegant rooms and spacious suites. Italian dishes are served in the hotel's restaurant, Via Sophia, while its microbar offers expertly crafted cocktails.

Henley Park Hotel

MAP Q3 ■ 926 Massachusetts Ave, NW ■ 202-638-5200 ■ www. henleypark.com ■ $

This Tudor-manor-style hotel boasts gargoyles on the outside and original stained glass and antique furniture inside.

Hotel Lombardy

MAP N3 ■ 2019 Pennsylvania Ave, NW ■ 202-828-2600 ■ www. hotellombardy.com ■ $

This hotel is decorated with imported fabrics, Oriental rugs, and original art. The Café Lombardy restaurant offers favorites such as crabcakes and grilled pork chops.

Tabard Inn

MAP N2 ■ 1739 N St, NW ■ 202-785-1277 ■ www. tabardinn.com ■ $

A boutique hotel, named for the inn in Chaucer's *Canterbury Tales*, this is converted from three townhouses. The rooms are charming and eclectic, and most have private baths. The restaurant serves superb American-Continental cuisine; the lounge-bar has live jazz.

Churchill Hotel

MAP M1 ■ 1914 Connecticut Ave, NW ■ 202-797-2000 ■ www. thechurchillhotel.com ■ $$

Opened as the Highlands apartment building in 1906, this grand Beaux Arts hotel between the Dupont Circle and Kalorama neighborhoods, boasts huge rooms.

Morrison House Old Town Alexandria

MAP C5 ■ 116 S Alfred St, Alexandria ■ 703-838-8000 ■ www.marriott. com ■ $$

This trendy Federal-style hotel in the center of Old Town offers upscale rooms while retaining the sophisticated historic details. The parlor and library are charming, and the onsite restaurant, The Study, offers locally sourced American fare.

Morrison-Clark Inn

MAP P3 ■ 1011 L St, NW ■ 202-898-1200 ■ www. morrisonclark.com ■ $$

Created by merging two townhouses, this mansion was the Soldiers', Sailors', Marines', and Airmen's Club for 50 years. Some of the original decorative touches still remain.

Phoenix Park Hotel

MAP R4 ■ 520 N Capitol St, NW ■ 202-638-6900 ■ www.phoenixparkhotel. com ■ $$

Named after the iconic park in Dublin, this hotel, set in a stately 1920s Georgian Revival building, has an Irish theme, right down to the live music and choice ales at the in-house pub.

Mayflower Hotel

MAP N3 ■ 1127 Connecticut Ave, NW ■ 202-347-3000 ■ www.marriott.com ■ $$

Opened in 1925 on the day of Calvin Coolidge's presidential inauguration, this hotel has hosted every Inaugural Ball since. Harry S. Truman stayed here during White House renovations; Franklin D. Roosevelt wrote his 1933 inaugural address here; and J. Edgar Hoover had lunch here most days.

Hay-Adams Hotel

MAP N3 ■ 800 16th, NW ■ 202-638-6600 ■ www. hayadams.com ■ $$$

Constructed on the sites of the homes of John Hay and Henry Adams, this elegant hotel features beautifully restored rooms furnished with antiques and ornamental ceilings.

The Jefferson

MAP N2 ■ 16th & M Sts, NW ■ 202-448-2300 ■ www.jeffersondc.com ■ $$$

The Jefferson's Beaux Arts facade is particularly eye-catching. The public areas feature displays of historic prints, paintings, and documents, including some associated with Thomas Jefferson. This elegant hotel is a popular choice with celebrities.

Mansion on O Street

MAP N2 ■ 2020 O St, NW ■ 202-496-2000 ■ www. omansion.com ■ $$$

This 100-room inn offers a variety of themed rooms, including a Graceland suite filled with memorabilia and the James Bond suite hidden behind a secret door (one of 70 on the property). The layout is so striking that guests often regard the house as a sight in itself. Eclectic and charming.

St. Regis Hotel

MAP N3 ■ 923 16th St, NW ■ 202-638-2626 ■ www.marriott.com ■ $$$

If both Queen Elizabeth II and the Rolling Stones chose to stay here, the St. Regis must be doing something right. The grand hotel is styled after a Renaissance palace and beautifully appointed with antiques, chandeliers, and fine tapestries.

Willard InterContinental

MAP P4 ■ 1401 Pennsylvania Ave, NW ■ 202-628-9100 ■ www.ihg.com ■ $$$

One of the most historic hotels in the city, this hotel has witnessed momentous world events, including the birth of the League of Nations, and royalty from all over the world have stayed here.

Boutique Hotels

citizenM Washington DC Capitol hotel

MAP Q5 ■ 550 School St, SW ■ 202-747-2145 ■ www.citizenm.com ■ $

Just south of the National Mall, this chain hotel offers a boutique experience for less cost, with simple but stylish rooms. The cloudM rooftop bar offers great views of the Capitol.

Hotel Hive

MAP M4 ■ 2224 F St, NW ■ 202-849-8499 ■ www. hotelhive.com ■ $

DC's first "micro hotel" offers good value given its central location, with small but beautifully designed rooms. You can enjoy pizzas and cocktails at the Hive Rooftop bar.

Capitol Hill Hotel

MAP S5 ■ 200 C St, SE ■ 202-543-6000 ■ www. capitolhillhotel–dc.com ■ $$

This suites-only hotel was recreated from an apartment building, and the result is spacious rooms with kitchens. It's located near the US Capitol and the Library of Congress, and Eastern Market.

Eaton DC

MAP P3 ■ 1201 K St, NW ■ 202-289-7600 ■ www. eatonworkshop.com ■ $$

Luxurious boutique hotel featuring eclectic decor that includes Scandi-inspired furniture and in-room LP turntables (with records to play).

Hotel Indigo Old Town Alexandria

MAP D5 ■ 220 S Union St, Alexandria ■ 703-721-3800 ■ www.ihg.com ■ $$

Great location just off the waterfront in the old town of Alexandria, with contemporary rooms (some with river views). There's an on-site fitness room and the Hummingbird Bar + Kitchen.

Hotel Madera

MAP N2 ■ 1310 New Hampshire Ave, NW ■ 202-296-7600 ■ www. hotelmadera.com ■ $$

Offering modern comfort with a stylish twist, this hotel exudes elegance and sophistication.

Royal Sonesta Washington DC

MAP M2 ■ 2121 P St, NW ■ 202-448-1800 ■ www.sonesta.com ■ $$

This boutique hotel offers luxury accommodations in a lively neighborhood. Some rooms have spa-style bathrooms.

Moxy Washington, DC Downtown

MAP P3 ■ 1011 K St, NW ■ 202-922-7400 ■ www. marriott.com ■ $$

Part of the Marriott stable, the Moxy is a chic blend of funky furniture and art with modern amenities. The lobby features board games and free coffee, while Bar Moxy serves hand-crafted cocktails and small plates, and has an outdoor terrace.

YOTEL Washington, DC

MAP R4 ■ 415 New Jersey Ave, NW ■ 202-638-1616 ■ www.yotel.com ■ $$

An elegant business boutique hotel with bright,

contemporary styling, an inviting rooftop pool and patio, and the farm-fresh, southern-inspired cuisine of Art and Soul Restaurant.

Kimpton George Hotel
MAP R4 ▪ 15 E St, NW ▪ 202-347-4200 ▪ www. hotelgeorge.com ▪ $$$
One of the most chic hotels in the city, the Kimpton George Hotel is deserving of the attention because of its innovative design and excellent business facilities. The French brasserie Bistro Bis offers dishes created by James Beard-award-winning chef Jeffrey Buben.

Kimpton Hotel Monaco
MAP Q4 ▪ 700 F St, NW ▪ 202-628-7177 ▪ www. monaco-dc.com ▪ $$$
Set in the 19th-century General Post Office building, the hotel has a stately facade and a colorful, modern interior. There's also an upscale library bar for after-hours.

Melrose Hotel
MAP M3 ▪ 2430 Pennsylvania Ave, NW ▪ 202-955-6400 ▪ www. melrosehoteldc.com ▪ $$$
A modern hotel in the heart of town, the Melrose is known for its refined luxury. The furnishings are contemporary but with classic influences.

Business Hotels

Embassy Suites – Georgetown
MAP M2 ▪ 1250 22nd St, NW ▪ 202-857-3388 ▪ www.hilton.com ▪ $
Part of the Hilton Group, Embassy Suites offers well-furnished bedrooms

with separate living areas. Conference rooms with extensive equipment are available for rent. There's also an indoor swimming pool and fitness center.

One Washington Circle Hotel
MAP M3 ▪ 1 Washington Circle, NW ▪ 202-872-1680 ▪ www.thecirclehotel.com ▪ $
Business travelers receive great service at this Foggy Bottom hotel. A knowledgeable staff manages the five meeting rooms, and suites have lots of seating space. Larger suites have full kitchens and walk-out balconies.

Courtyard Washington Convention Center
MAP Q4 ▪ 900 F St, NW ▪ 202-638-4600 ▪ www. marriott.com ▪ $$
Situated in a former 1891 bank but completely updated with an indoor pool and fitness center. The hotel has two conference rooms.

Courtyard Washington, DC Dupont Circle
MAP N2 ▪ 1733 N St, NW ▪ 202-393-3000 ▪ www. marriott.com ▪ $$
Located in a quiet area of Dupont Circle, this hotel offers complimentary continental breakfast, yoga mats and public bikes. The bar is among the best in the city.

Homewood Suites
MAP P2 ▪ 1475 Massachusetts Ave, NW ▪ 202-265-8000 ▪ www.hilton. com ▪ $$
This 175-room hotel is ideal for extended stays as it is centrally located

and offers good-sized accommodations, with separate living and sleeping areas and full kitchen. A free hot breakfast is served daily, and there are laundry facilities and a 24/7 convenience store.

Renaissance Washington, DC Downtown
MAP Q3 ▪ 999 9th St, NW ▪ 202-898-9000 ▪ www. marriott.com ▪ $$
This large hotel, with over 800 rooms, is hard to miss thanks to its striking glass facade. It may be oriented toward catering to business travelers, but is set in an excellent tourist location in Penn Quarter. It also features spas and business centers, a library in the lobby, and several dining options to choose from, including the Liberty Market deli.

Hilton Washington DC Capitol Hill
MAP R4 ▪ 525 New Jersey Ave, NW ▪ 202-628-2100 ▪ www.hilton.com ▪ $$
The rooms at this hotel are sleek and modern, with free Wi-Fi and flat-screen TVs. Some have stunning views of the US Capitol. The hotel is close to Union Station.

Washington Marriott at Metro Center
MAP P3 ▪ 775 12th St, NW ▪ 202-737-2200 ▪ www.marriott.com ▪ $$
Benefitting greatly from its central downtown location, this modern hotel provides guests with a personal touch despite its large size with 459 rooms and suites. The Fire and Sage restaurant serves seasonal food.

For a key to hotel price categories see p126

Capital Hilton

MAP N3 ■ 1001 16th St at K St, NW ■ 202-393-1000 ■ www.hilton.com ■ $$$

This hotel is in a great location, just two blocks from the White House, and offers all state-of-the-art meeting facilities offered by the Hilton chain, plus a health club and spa.

Washington Hilton

MAP N1 ■ 1919 Connecticut Ave, NW ■ 202-483-3000 ■ www.hilton.com ■ $$$

The garden setting is lovely, and the elevated location gives a fine view of the city skyline. The complex's layout and size and its rooftop pool and sun deck make for a resort-like atmosphere.

The Westin Georgetown

MAP M3 ■ 2350 M St NW ■ 202-429-0100 ■ www.marriott.com ■ $$$

Marble bathrooms with extra-deep bathtubs are among the amenities here. There is an outdoor pool and a leafy courtyard garden, with a choice of the Caucus Room French brasserie or the Latin-American Bóveda tavern for in-house dining. Dogs are permitted.

The Westin Washington DC City Center

MAP N2 ■ 1400 M St NW ■ 202-429-1700 ■ www.marriott.com ■ $$$

A large hotel with two full-service restaurants, plus an on-site Starbucks. Located four blocks from the McPherson Metro and nearby Logan Circle, the Westin has a large central atrium and all the expected business amenities. The hotel also provides a 24-hour fitness center, and is pet-friendly.

Mid-Range Hotels

Embassy Suites Hotel at the Chevy Chase Pavilion

MAP G2 ■ 4300 Military Rd, NW (at Wisconsin & Western Aves) ■ 202-362-9300 ■ www.hilton.com ■ $

Situated in the popular Chevy Chase shopping mall, this all-suites hotel has easy access to a wide range of shops and restaurants, as well as the Friendship Heights Metro. Breakfast is included in the tariff, and complimentary drinks and appetizers are served at a two-hour reception in Willie's Bar every evening.

Georgetown House

MAP L3 ■ 1061 31st St, NW ■ 202-827-4294 ■ www.thegeorgetownhousedc.com ■ $

This cozy inn offers great value, close to the main drag in Georgetown. The main part of the inn was built in the 1830s as a warehouse for the C&O canal, and later served as a tavern and stable.

Motto by Hilton Washington DC City Center

MAP Q3 ■ 627 H St, NW ■ 202-847-4444 ■ www.hilton.com ■ $

Stylish contemporary hotel in Chinatown, with compact, modern rooms. The Crimson View bar has a stellar outdoor terrace overlooking the Washington Monument (perfect for drinks at sunset) and the Crimson Diner & Coffee Bar serves up locally roasted coffee.

Beacon Hotel and Corporate Quarters

MAP N2 ■ 1615 Rhode Island Ave, NW (at 17th St) ■ 202-296-2100 ■ www.beaconhotelwdc.com ■ $$

The very comfortable rooms are decorated with cosmopolitan flair. Eight deluxe turret suites and 60 corporate suites come with fully equipped kitchens, high-speed internet and web TV. The Beacon Bar & Grill restaurant serves food all day, from breakfast to dinner.

Crystal City Marriott at Reagan National Airport

MAP D4 ■ 1999 Jefferson Davis Highway, Arlington VA ■ 703-413-5500 ■ www.marriott.com ■ $$

This hotel offers simple yet stylish rooms and classic American dishes at its BELL20 restaurant. It also provides a shuttle to the nearby Reagan National Airport.

Georgetown Inn

MAP L2 ■ 1310 Wisconsin Ave, NW ■ 202-333-8900 ■ www.georgetowninn.com ■ $$

This hotel opened in 1961 at the height of John F. Kennedy's administration and the public's interest in Georgetown glamor, and it has been a permanent fixture on the Washington hotel scene ever since. All rooms are large and decorated in tasteful, elegant style, and offer free Wi-Fi. This hotel has a 24-hour exercise room and provides free passes to a local fitness center, located nearby.

West End part of the Georgetown Collection

MAP M3 ■ 1121 New Hampshire Ave, NW ■ 202-457-0565 ■ georgetowninnwest end.com ■ $$
With a location equidistant from the White House, historic Georgetown and the lively Dupont Circle neighborhood, this bou-tique hotel is quickly becoming a favorite with both families and businesspeople. A free continental breakfast is served daily. Children 17 and under stay free.

Hotel Harrington

MAP P4 ■ 11th & E Sts, NW ■ 202-628-8140 ■ www. hotel-harrington.com ■ $$
At one time, this was the largest hotel in the city. A century later, it is still run by members of the found-ing family. It is popular with school groups, and also has some family suites with two bathrooms each.

The Normandy Hotel

MAP M1 ■ 2118 Wyoming Ave, NW ■ 202-483-1350 ■ www.thenormandydc. com ■ $$
Located on a peaceful residential street, the Normandy hotel has the feel of a classic bed and breakfast. Complimentary wine and quality cheese are served to guests on Tuesday nights, and coffee, tea, and cookies are offered at other times.

The River Inn

MAP N1 ■ 924 25th St, NW ■ 202-337-7600 ■ www.theriverinn.com ■ $$
This popular hotel in Foggy Bottom has 126 suites, each with a full kitchen and a work or dining area. The River Inn also pro-vides bikes for exploring the nearby C&O Canal.

State Plaza Hotel

MAP M4 ■ 2117 E St, NW ■ 202-861-8200 ■ www. stateplaza.com ■ $$
This chic all-suites hotel, conveniently located between the White House and the Kennedy Center, features a bistro with out-door seating, a rooftop sun deck, and a fitness center. Suites come with kitchens and have high-speed internet access.

Family-Friendly Hotels

Holiday Inn Central

MAP P2 ■ 1501 Rhode Island Ave at 15th St, NW ■ 202-483-2000 ■ www. ihg.com ■ $
This hotel has a rooftop pool, cable TV, and in-room movies that will keep children entertained. Some oversized rooms are available for families. The Dupont Circle and McPherson Square Metro stops are located within walking distance.

Omni Shoreham Hotel

MAP M1 ■ 2500 Calvert St, NW (at Connecticut Ave) ■ 202-234-0700 ■ www. omnihotels.com ■ $
Set close to Rock Creek Park and the National Zoo, the Omni Shoreham Hotel's location makes it ideal for travelers with

children. All its young guests are provided with interesting activity backpacks on check-in.

Residence Inn Alexandria Old Town/Duke Street

MAP C5 ■ 1456 Duke St, Alexandria ■ 703-548-5474 ■ www.marriott. com ■ $
Set just outside the old center of Alexandria, this justly popular pet-friendly hotel offers excellent value, with spacious rooms, free coffee, and a laundry on-site (coin-operated). Crucially, all rooms and suites come with kitchens, and cribs and baby play pens are also available.

Washington Plaza

MAP P2 ■ 10 Thomas Circle, NW ■ 202-842-1300 ■ www.washington plaza hotel.com ■ $
The large resort-like hotel and its beautifully landscaped grounds surround a large open-air swimming pool. Guests at this establish-ment can enjoy poolside dining during the sum-mer, and a lounge with an open fire pit during the winter.

Fairfield Inn and Suites

MAP Q3 ■ 500 H St, NW ■ 202-289-5959 ■ www. marriott.com ■ $$
This hotel is better suited to cater to the needs of the business traveler. However, prices are still reasonable, the staff are great, and the suites are a good choice for family stays. The hotel is within easy reach of the Capital One Arena.

For a key to hotel price categories see p126

Hampton Inn and Suites National Harbor/ Alexandria Area

MAP D6 ▪ 250 Waterfront Street, Oxon Hill, MD ▪ 301-567-3531 ▪ www. hilton.com ▪ $$

Located just a block away from the Potomac river with a carousel and a giant Ferris wheel set two blocks away, the Hampton Inn & Suites is very child-friendly. Amenities here include an indoor pool, free hot breakfast, and Wi-Fi. The location is handy for exploring Mount Vernon and historic Old Town Alexandria by water taxi.

Holiday Inn Washington Capitol - Natl Mall

MAP Q5 ▪ 550 C St, SW ▪ 202-479-4000 ▪ www. ihg.com ▪ $$

This Holiday Inn offers an outdoor rooftop pool with a view; it is just one block away from the Air and Space Museum; and kids under 12 can eat for free. In addition, there is a Starbucks on-site. The hotel also provides guests with laundry facilities.

J.W. Marriott

MAP P4 ▪ 1331 Pennsylvania Ave, NW ▪ 202-393-2000 ▪ www. marriott.com ▪ $$

Located only two blocks away from the White House and set close to the National Mall and the fun International Spy Museum, this hotel has a great location that mini- mizes walking distances for little feet. Childcare is also offered by prior arrangement. A fitness center is also available. Free Wi-Fi in public areas.

Hilton Washington, DC National Mall

MAP Q5 ▪ 480 L'Enfant Plaza, SW ▪ 202-484- 1000 ▪ www.hilton.com ▪ $$$

This hotel is close to the kid-friendly International Spy Museum and less than a 10-minute walk to the National Mall, a large grassy park. The contem- porary decor is dazzling.

Budget Hotels

Capital Square BNB

MAP D4 ▪ 1259 K St, SE ▪ 240-781-8270 ▪ $

This budget spot, found just a block away from the Potomac Avenue Metro station, is more like a hostel than a B&B, with male-only, female-only, and mixed dorms, plus private rooms (with one twin bed and one double bed). All rooms have shared bathrooms. A simple breakfast and free coffee and tea are served daily.

Days Inn

MAP H3 ▪ 4400 Connecticut Ave NW, Van Ness ▪ 202-244-5600 ▪ www.wyndhamhotels. com ▪ $

A convenient, affordable hotel, north of Cleveland Park near the Van Ness Metro, with clean rooms. Several restaurants are located nearby, including the Tesoro next door, which serves authentic Italian cuisine.

Duo Housing

MAP P2 ▪ 1223 11th St, NW ▪ 202-808-2195 ▪ www.duohousing.com ▪ $

This decent hostel is located in the hip Logan Circle neighborhood,

with a spread of extras: free Wi-Fi, shared Nintendo Wii, cable TV, a kitchen offering free coffee and tea, and flexible check-in times 24/7. There's also a superb roof deck with views across the city.

Duo Nomad

MAP D4 ▪ 1010 Pennsylvania Ave, SE ▪ 202-629-3495 ▪ www. duonomad.com ▪ $

Another hostel in the Duo collection, this one is close to Barracks Row and Eastern Market. Like its sister hostel, there's a 24/7 front desk, and free Wi-Fi, coffee and tea. It also has a shared kitchen and an outdoor terrace.

Generator Washington DC

MAP M1 ▪ 1900 Connecticut Ave, NW ▪ 202-332-9300 ▪ www. staygenerator.com ▪ $

Conveniently located close to Adams Morgan, this hip budget hotel from the Generator stable is known for its bright colors, contemporary style, and fun club nights. Extras include bike hire, a rooftop terrace and an outdoor pool.

Holiday Inn Arlington at Ballston

MAP D4 ▪ 4610 Fairfax Dr, Arlington ▪ 703-243- 9800 ▪ www.ihg.com ▪ $

One of the best-value chain motels on the outskirts of DC (it's just 5 miles west of the National Mall, and a short walk from Ballston- MU Metro). Rooms are standard but comfy and modern with all the usual amenities, including coffee makers. There's also an on-site restaurant and a fitness center.

U Street Hostel

MAP P1 ▪ 1931 13th St, NW ▪ 202-892-1122 ▪ www.ustreethostel. com ▪ $

This hostel is found just off the U Street corridor of restaurants and bars, across from Ben's Chili Bowl (see p112). It offers Japanese-style "capsule" pods (with lights, work table, and USB ports) in addition to the usual bunks, with shared bathrooms. There are also private rooms with ensuite bathrooms.

Bed and Breakfast

The American Guest House

MAP N1 ▪ 2005 Columbia Rd, NW ▪ 202-588-1180 ▪ www.americanguest house.com ▪ $

Set in a colonial-style townhouse dating from 1898, this charming guesthouse provides a comfortable base for travelers in the elegant Kalorama neighborhood. The 12 well-maintained rooms, with Wi-Fi, are handsomely furnished with wood floors, Oriental carpets, and period furnishings and artwork. A free homemade breakfast is offered daily.

The Inn at Dupont South

MAP N2 ▪ 1312 19th St, NW ▪ 202-359-8432 ▪ www.thedupontcollec tion.com ▪ $

Set just south of Dupont Circle, the Inn occupies a Victorian row house dating to 1855. Most of the bedrooms have a

private bath and fireplace, and all have air-conditioning and wireless internet access. There's a private walled garden in which to enjoy a relaxing afternoon tea.

Kalorama Guest House

MAP J4 ▪ 2700 Cathedral Ave, NW ▪ 202-588-8188 ▪ www.kalorama guesthouse.com ▪ $

Cozy B&B set across two buildings on a quiet tree-lined street not far from the National Zoos (see p112). It has friendly owners and worn but clean rooms. Continental breakfast is served, along with a spread of snacks. The cheaper rooms have shared bathrooms.

Ledroit Park Bed and Breakfast

MAP R1 ▪ 210 T St, NW ▪ 202-277-7847 ▪ www. ledroitparkrennaissance bedandbreakfast.com ▪ $

A restored 1890 row house with Victorian-era furnishings, this B&B is located in the LeDroit neighborhood, once home to the first educated and professional African Americans of the time. It is close to the U Street (see p112) with its many shops and restaurants.

The Oaks B&B

MAP B1 ▪ 9201 Laurel Oak Dr, Bethesda, MD ▪ 202-681-4466 ▪ www. oaksbnb.com ▪ $

This B&B lies in a tranquil residential section of Bethesda, just off I-495 some 12 miles northwest of the National Mall (you'll need a car to make the most of this location). The four guest rooms

are beautifully designed, the owners are a font of useful local knowledge, and the full breakfasts are superb.

Akwaaba Bed & Breakfast

MAP N2 ▪ 1708 16th St, NW ▪ 866-466-3855 ▪ www.akwaaba.com ▪ $$

This bed and breakfast is within walking distance of the White House. The historic townhouse has eight ensuite rooms, featuring premium linens, cable TV, and free Wi-Fi. Some rooms have a private balcony, Jacuzzi tub, and a decorative fireplace.

Woodley Park Guest House

MAP J5 ▪ 2647 Woodley Rd, NW ▪ 202-667-0218 ▪ www.woodleypark guesthouse.com ▪ $$

This family-oriented bed and breakfast features airy, comfortable rooms, decorated with tasteful furnishings and collector art. The buffet breakfast will keep everyone going till lunch at the nearby National Zoo (see p112). The National Cathedral (see pp30–31) and Metro are also close by.

Swann House

MAP N1 ▪ 1808 New Hampshire Ave, NW ▪ 202-265-4414 ▪ www. swannhouse.com ▪ $$$

Sometimes described as the best bed and breakfast in the city, this inviting 1883 mansion combines sparkling chandeliers and open fireplaces with all modern conveniences – Wi-Fi, private baths, and cable TV, and even a pool. Breakfast includes their homemade granola and gourmet hot dishes.

General Index

Page numbers in **bold** refer to Top 10 highlights.

1789 Restaurant 69, 109

A

Abakanowicz, Magdalena 27
Accommodations 125
bed and breakfast 133
hotels 126–33
Adams, Abigail 19, 104
Adams, John 19, 44
Adoration of the Magi, The (Angelico) 24
African American Civil War Memorial and Museum 47, 51, 112
African American history 46–7
Air travel 118, 119
Alba Madonna, The (Raphael) 25
Alcohol 122
Alleys, Capitol Hill 82
Ambulances 123
Amendments, US Constitution 43
American Indians National Museum of the American Indian 7, 54, 85, 89
American Veterans Disabled for Life Memorial 82
Amusement parks
Six Flags America and Hurricane Harbor 64
Anacostia Museum and Center for African American History and Culture 46
Anderson, Lars 49
Anderson, Marion 47
Anderson House 49
Angelico, Fra 24
Annapolis, Maryland 74
Anthony, Susan B. 15
Architecture 49, 70, 100
Arena Stage 66

Arlington House 34, 35
Arlington National Cemetery 7, 11, **34–5**, 111
Art galleries *see* Museums and galleries
Arthur M. Sackler Gallery 57
Assateague, Virginia 74

B

Bacon, Henry 86
Ball, Thomas 47
Baltimore, Maryland 74
Banks 124
Bartholdi, Frédéric Auguste 59
Bartholdi Park and Fountain 59, 80
Baseball 61
Basilica of the National Shrine of the Immaculate Conception 111
Basketball 61
Bed and breakfast 125, 133
Belmont-Paul House 49, 81
Berks, Robert 47, 51
Bethesda, Maryland 113
Bethune, Mary McLeod 46–7, 49, 82
Beyond the City Center 110–15
map 110
restaurants 115
shopping 114
Bicycles 60, 121
Bingham, George Caleb 18, 24
Blue Duck Tavern 68, 103
Boating 60
river cruises 38
Tidal Basin 90
Booth, John Wilkes 48, 95
Bourgeois, Louise 27
Brown, John 74

Brumidi, Constantino 12, 15
Budget travel 70–71
hotels 132–3
Bulfinch, Charles 14
Bunche, Ralph 47
Bureau of Engraving and Printing 71, 88
Burton, Scott 27
Buses 118, 119, 121, 123
Bus tours 120

C

Calder, Alexander 24
Canal, Chesapeake and Ohio 58, 105, 107
Capital Jazz Fest 72
Capital One Arena 61, 67, 95
Capital Wheel at National Harbor 64
Capitol see US Capitol
Capitol Grounds 82
Capitol Hill 78–83
map 78–9
residences 80, 82
restaurants 83
Cappellano, Antonio 15
Carnegie, Andrew 48
Carnegie Library 48
Cars 71
car rental 120
driving 120
gasoline (petrol) 120–21
parking 120
rules of the road 121
Carter Barron Amphitheatre 67
Cathedrals
Washington National Cathedral 7, 11, **30–31**, 73, 111, 112
see also Churches
Causici, Enrico 12
Cemetery, Arlington National 7, 11, **34–5**, 111
Central Michel Richard 68, 91

Chagall, Marc 106
Chesapeake and Ohio
Canal 58, 105, 107
Child, Julia 22, 85
Children's attractions
64–5, 90
Children's Theater 65, 70
Chinatown 96
Chincoteague, Virginia
74
Chinese New Year 73
Christ Church 82, 113
Christmas Tree lighting
73
Church, Frederick Edwin
25
Churches
Basilica of the
National Shrine
of the Immaculate
Conception 111
Christ Church 82, 113
Ebenezer United
Methodist Church 82
Grace Church 106–7
Metropolitan African
Methodist Episcopal
Church 46
Mount Zion United
Methodist Church 47
see also Cathedrals
Churchill, Winston 16, 51
Cinema see Films
Circulator see DC
Circulator
Citi Open 61
Civil War 14, 35, 42
African American Civil
War Memorial and
Museum 47, 51, 112,
116–17
Gettysburg 75
Manassas Battlefield
75
Clara Barton Missing
Soldiers Office
Museum 95
Cleveland, Frances 22
Climbing 61
Clinton, Bill 50
Clinton, Hillary 45
Cluss, Adolph 81
Colonial Williamsburg 75

Columbus, Christopher
13
Constitution Gardens 88
Constitution Hall 67,
100–101
Coolidge, Calvin 45
Coolidge, Grace 45
Coolidge Auditorium 67
Copley, John Singleton
24
Corcoran School of the
Arts and Design 101
COVID-19 124
Cox's Row 49
Crawford, Thomas 15
Credit cards 124
Cret, Paul Philippe 79
Crime 123
Currency 124
Custis, Nelly 36
Customs information
122, 123
Cycling 60, 121

D

Dance Lesson, The
(Degas) 26
Daughters of the
American Revolution
(DAR) 100–101
Davis, Jefferson 15
DC Circulator 106, 119
DC United 61
Decatur, Stephen 48
Decatur House 48, 101,
102
Degas, Edgar 26, 27, 56
Dining see Restaurants
Distillery, George
Washington's 7, 39, 63
Doctors 122, 123
Douglass, Anna 46, 49
Douglass, Frederick 46,
49
Driving see Cars
Drugs 122
Dumbarton Oaks 7, 49,
59, 105
Dunbar, Paul Lawrence
47
Dwight D. Eisenhower
Office Building 49,
101

E

East Building (National
Gallery of Art) 24–5,
27
East Potomac Park 59
Eastern Market 69, 80
Ebenezer United
Methodist Church 82
Einstein, Albert 51
El Greco 26, 105
Electrical appliances
124
Ellington, Duke 47, 112
Emancipation
Monument 82
Emergency services
123
Enid A. Haupt Garden
58
Entertainment 66–7, 71
Evans, Rudolph 50

F

Farrand, Beatrix Jones
59
Fashion Centre at
Pentagon City, The 69
Festivals 72–3
Films
Filmfest DC 73
free performances 73
Lockheed Martin IMAX
Theater 90
Fire services 123
First Division Monument
51
First Ladies 45
Flanagan, Barry 27
Folger Shakespeare
Library and Theatre
66, 79, 81
Food and drink
budget travel 71
National Capitol
Barbecue Battle 72
see also Restaurants
Football 61
Ford's Theatre 48, 66, 95
Foster, Norman 96
Franklin, Benjamin 51
Franklin D. Roosevelt
Memorial 50, 87, 88
Frederick, Maryland 75

Frederick Douglass National Historic Site 46, 49
Fredericksburg, Virginia 75
Free Washington 70–71
Freer Gallery of Art 57
French, Daniel Chester 50, 86
Friendship Heights 69

G

Gadsby's Tavern Museum 48, 113
GALA Hispanic Theatre 67
Galleries see Museums and galleries
Gardens see Parks and gardens
George Mason Memorial 62
George Washington University 100
George Washington University Museum and The Textile Museum, The 89, 99
George Washington's Distillery 7, 39, 63
Georgetown 5, 7, 76–7, 104–9
    map 104
    restaurants 109
    shopping 69, 108
Georgetown University 106
Georgetown University Basketball 61
Georgetown Waterfront Park 63, 106
Gettysburg, Pennsylvania 75
Gilbert, Cass 80
Ginevra de' Benci (Leonardo da Vinci) 24
Girl with the Red Hat (Vermeer) 24
Golf 60–61
Government advice 122
Grace Church 106–7
Great Falls 113

H

Hamilton, Ed 51
Harman Center for the Arts 67
Harpers Ferry, West Virginia 74
Harriman, Averell 106
Hart, Frederick 30
Haupt (Enid A.) Garden 58
Health 122, 123
Hiking 61
Hirshhorn Museum and Sculpture Garden 56, 85
Historic homes and buildings 48–9
History 42–3, 46–7
Hockey 61
Home Rule Charter (1973) 43
Homer, Winslow 25, 96
Horse racing 73
Horseback riding 61
Hospitals 122, 123
Hotels 125–33
    boutique hotels 128–9
    budget hotels 71, 132–3
    business hotels 129–30
    family-friendly hotels 131–2
    historic hotels 127–8
    luxury hotels 126–7
    mid-range hotels 130–31

I

Ice skating 90
ID 122
In-line skating 60
Independence Day 73
Insurance 122
International Gold Cup Steeplechase Races 73
International Spy Museum 55, 65, 88
Internet 124, 125
Iron Gate 69, 103
Iwo Jima Statue (Marine Corps Memorial) 51

J

Jackson, Andrew 18, 44, 51, 101
Jackson, Jesse 46
Jamestown 75
Jazz 72
Jefferson, Thomas 44
    Declaration of Independence 23
    Jefferson Memorial 6, 7, 50, 87, 88
    Lewis and Clark expedition 42
    Library of Congress 79
Jefferson Building 70
Jefferson Memorial 6, 7, 50, 87, 88
Jews
    United States Holocaust Memorial Museum 54–5, 86–7, 90–1
Jiffy Lube Live 67
Joan of Arc 51
Johnson, Adelaide 15
Johnson, Lady Bird 45
Johnson, Lyndon B. 45
Johnson, Philip 105
Jouvenal, Jacques 51

K

Kenilworth Park and Aquatic Gardens 59, 62
Kennedy, Jacqueline 19, 22, 35, 45, 89, 106
Kennedy, John F. 45, 86, 99, 109
    grave 34, 35
Kennedy Center 5, 6, 66, 70, 99, 101
King, Martin Luther, Jr 16, 47
    Lincoln Memorial 46
    March on Washington 43
    Martin Luther King, Jr. Day 73
    Martin Luther King, Jr. Memorial 46

King, Martin Luther, Jr (cont.)
  Metropolitan African Methodist Episcopal Church 46
Kites 73
Komi 69, 103
Korean War Veterans Memorial 51, 88
Kreeger Museum 57

L

Lafayette, Marquis de 14, 37, 101
Lafayette Park 16, 101
Language 125
Lee, Robert E. 35
Lei Yixin 46
L'Enfant, Pierre Charles 14, 34, 42, 100
Leonardo da Vinci 24
Lewis and Clark expedition 19, 42
LeWitt, Sol 27
Libraries
  Carnegie Library 48
  Folger Shakespeare Library 79, 81
  Library of Congress 6, 40–41, 49, 70, 79, 81
  White House 18
Lichtenstein, Roy 27
Lin, Maya 50, 86
Lincoln, Abraham 44
  assassination 23, 45, 62, 66, 95
  Emancipation Monument 47, 82
  Ford's Theatre 48, 66, 95
  Gettysburg Address 75
  Lincoln Memorial 5, 6, 7, 46, 50, 86
  statue of 51
  White House 17
Lincoln, Mary Todd 45
Lincoln Memorial 5, 6, 7, 46, 50, 86
Lincoln Park 47
Lincoln Theatre 67
Lindbergh, Charles 21
Lippi, Filippo 24
Lisner Auditorium 67

Local Customs 125
Lockheed Martin IMAX Theater 90
Lockkeeper's House 62

M

M Street 105
McMillan Plan 43
McVey, William M. 51
Madame Tussauds 90
Madison, Dolley 45
Madison, James 44, 100
Mail 124
Manassas Battlefield 75
Manship, Paul 51
Maps 6–7
  around Capitol Hill 78–9
  art galleries 57
  beyond the City Center 110
  Georgetown 104
  museums 55
  National Mall, The 84–5
  off the beaten path 63
  Penn Quarter 94
  restaurants 68
  trips from Washington, DC 75
  Washington, DC's highlights 10–11
  White House and Foggy Bottom 98–9
Marcel's 69, 103
Marie Antoinette, Queen 28
Marine Corps Memorial (Iwo Jima Statue) 51
Martin Luther King, Jr. Day 73
Martin Luther King, Jr. Memorial 46
Mary McLeod Bethune Council House 46–7, 49
Mason, George 62
Memorial Day 73
Memorials and monuments 50–51
  African American Civil War Memorial and Museum 47, 51, 112, 116–17

Memorials and monuments (cont.)
  American Veterans Disabled for Life Memorial 82
  Emancipation Monument 47, 82
  First Division Monument 51
  Franklin D. Roosevelt Memorial 50, 87, 88
  George Mason Memorial 62
  Iwo Jima Statue (Marine Corps Memorial) 51
  Jefferson Memorial 6, 7, 50, 87, 88
  Korean War Veterans Memorial 51, 88
  Lincoln Memorial 5, 6, 7, 46, 50, 86
  Martin Luther King, Jr. Memorial 46
  Robert A. Taft Memorial 82
  Rough Riders Monument 35
  Seabees Memorial 35
  Tomb of the Unknown Soldier 34
  Ulysses S. Grant Memorial 51, 82
  Vietnam Veterans Memorial 7, 50–51, 86
  Washington Monument 5, 6, 7, 50, 87
  World War II Memorial 51, 88
Metrobus 118, 119
Metropolitan African Methodist Episcopal Church 46
Metrorail 71, 106, 118, 119, 123, 124
Mills, Clark 51
Miró, Joan 27
Mobile phones 124
Monet, Claude 26, 57
Money 124
Monroe, James 5, 18, 19
Mott, Lucretia 15
Mount Vernon 7, 11, **36–9**, 111

Mount Zion United Methodist Church 47
Museums and galleries 54–6
opening hours 124
shopping 89
Anacostia Museum and Center for African American History and Culture 46
Arthur M. Sackler Gallery 57, 89
Colonial Williamsburg 75
Corcoran Gallery of Art 99, 101
Dumbarton Oaks 49, 105
Freer Gallery of Art 57
Gadsby's Tavern Museum 48, 113
George Washington University Museum and The Textile Museum, The 89, 99
Hirshhorn Museum and Sculpture Garden 56, 85
International Spy Museum 55, 65, 88
Kreeger Museum 57
Lockkeeper's House 62
Mount Vernon 39
National Air and Space Museum 6, 7, 10, **20–21**, 54, 64, 85, 89, 90, 112
National Archives of the United States 55, 70, 88
National Building Museum 49, 95
National Gallery of Art 5, 6, 10, **24–7**, 56, 85, 89, 90
National Geographic Museum 63, 101
National Guard Memorial Museum 82

Museum and galleries (cont.)
National Museum of African American History and Culture **32–33**, 47, 55, 85
National Museum of African Art 57, 88
National Museum of American History 6, 10, **22–3**, 54, 65, 85
National Museum of the American Indian 7, 54, 85, 89
National Museum of Health and Medicine 62
National Museum of Natural History 5, 6, 7, 11, **28–9**, 54, 65, 86, 89
National Museum of Women in the Arts 57, 96
National Portrait Gallery 56, 96
National Postal Museum 55, 62, 81
National Sculpture Garden 6
Octagon Museum 49, 100
Old Stone House 49, 62, 107
Oxon Hill Farm 64–5
The Phillips Collection 56
Renwick Gallery 56, 99, 101
Sewall-Belmont House 49, 80–81
Smithsonian American Art Museum 96
Stabler-Leadbeater Apothecary Museum 113
Tudor Place 107
United States Holocaust Memorial Museum 54–5, 86–7, 90
Woodrow Wilson House 48
Music 70, 72, 73

N
N Street 106
National Air and Space Museum 10, **20–21**, 54, 85
children's attractions 64, 90
exploring Washington, DC 6, 7
Steven F. Udar-Hazy Center 112
store 89
National Arboretum 58, 71
National Archives of the United States 55, 70, 88
National Book Festival 73
National Building Museum 49, 95
National Capitol Barbecue Battle 72
National Cherry Blossom Festival 72
National Gallery of Art 5, 10, **24–7**, 56, 85
children's attractions 90
exploring Washington, DC 6
shop 89
National Geographic Museum 63, 101
National Guard Memorial Museum 82
National Harbour 69, 114
National Law Enforcement Museum 55
National Mall, The 5, 84–91
children's attractions 90
items in museum stores 89
map 84–5
restaurants 91
National Museum of African American History and Culture **32–33**, 47, 55, 85

National Museum of African Art 57, 88
National Museum of American History 10, **22–3**, 54, 85
children's attractions 65
exploring Washington, DC 6
shop 89
National Museum of the American Indian 7, 54, 85, 89
National Museum of Health and Medicine 62
National Museum of Natural History 5, 11, **28–9**, 54, 86
children's attractions 65
exploring Washington, DC 6, 7
O. Orkin Insect Zoo 28, 90
shop 89
National Museum of Women in the Arts 57, 96
National Portrait Gallery 56, 96
National Postal Museum 55, 62, 81
National Symphony Labor Day Concert 73
National Theatre 67
National Zoo 7, 11, 64, 70, **112**
Nationals Park 67
Naval Academy Football 61
Neptune Fountain 51
New Deal 43
Nixon, Richard 19
Norton, Eleanor Holmes 47

O
Obama, Barack 19, 45
Obama, Michelle 22, 45
Obelisk 68, 103
Octagon Museum 49, 100
Old Post Office Tower 49

Old Stone House 49, 62, 107
Old Town Alexandria 7, 111
Olmsted, Frederick Law 82
Opening hours 124
O. Orkin Insect Zoo 28, 54, 90
Outdoor activities 60–61
Oxon Hill Farm 64–5

P
Paca, William 74
Paine, Roxy 27
Parks and gardens 58–9
Bartholdi Park and Fountain 59, 80
Bishop's Garden 31
Capitol Grounds 82
Constitution Gardens 88
Dumbarton Oaks 49, 59, 105
East Potomac Park 59
Enid A. Haupt Garden 58
Georgetown Water-front Park 63, 106
Hirshhorn Museum and Sculpture Garden 85
Kenilworth Park and Aquatic Gardens 59 62,
Lafayette Park 101
Lincoln Park 47
Mount Vernon 39
National Arboretum 58, 71
National Cherry Blossom Festival 72
Rock Creek Park 58–9
Theodore Roosevelt Island 59
US Botanic Garden 6, 58, 71, 80
Parks, Rosa 46
Passports 122, 123
Peale, Charles Willson 36
Peirce Mill 63

Penn Quarter 6, 69, 94–7
map 94
restaurants 97
Pennsylvania Avenue 96
Pentagon, The 51
Perry, Roland Hinton 51
Personal security 123
Peter family 107
Pharmacies 122, 123, 124
Phillips Collection, The 56
Pickersgill, Mary 23
Pinkerton, Alan 96
Pocahontas 15
Police 123
Polk, James K. 45
Polk, Sarah 45
Pope, John Russell 24, 100–101
Pope-Leighey House 49
Portraits of the First Five Presidents (Stuart) 25
Postal services 124, 125
National Postal Museum 55, 62, 81
Potomac Mills Mall 69
Potomac River 38, 59, 60, 113
Presidents 44–5
Public transportation 118, 119
Tickets 118

R
Railways 118, 119
Raphael 25, 26
Rasika 69, 97
Reagan, Nancy 22
Refunds 125
Renwick, James, Jr. 99
Renwick Gallery 56, 99, 101
Restaurants 68
around Capitol Hill 83
beyond the City Center 115
Georgetown 109
National Mall, The 91
Penn Quarter 97
White House and Foggy Bottom 103
see also Food and drink

Reynolds, George G. 30
Right and Left (Homer) 25
River of Light, The (Church) 25
Robert A. Taft Memorial 82
Rock Creek Park 58–9
Rogers, Randolph 13, 15
Roosevelt, Eleanor 45
Roosevelt, Franklin D. 44, 47, 86
   Franklin D. Roosevelt Memorial 50, 87, 88
   Georgetown 104
   New Deal 43
   White House 16, 19
Roosevelt, Theodore 44, 89
   statue of 51, 59
   Theodore Roosevelt Island 59
   Washington National Cathedral 31
Rough Riders Monument 35
Running 60

S

Sackler (Arthur M.) Gallery 57, 89
Safety 122, 123
St. John's Church 99
St. Patrick's Day 73
Samaras, Lucas 27
Screen on the Green 71
Seabees Memorial 35
Shakespeare, William 66
   Folger Shakespeare Library and Theatre 79, 81
   Shakespeare Free for All 72
   Shakespeare Theatre 66
Shaw, WB 59
Shopping 69
   beyond the City Center 114
   Georgetown 108

Shopping (cont.)
   museum stores 89
   opening hours 124
Shops at National Place, The 69
Shrady, Henry Merwin 51, 82
Six Flags America and Hurricane Harbor 64
Skating
   ice skating 90
   in-line skating 60
Skyline Drive, Virginia 74
Smith, Tony 27
Smithson, James 29
Smithsonian American Art Museum 96
Smithsonian Institution 29
   Arthur M. Sackler Gallery 57, 89
   Blossom Kite Festival 73
   Carousel on the Mall 65, 90
   Live Butterfly Pavilion 29, 65, 90
   Enid A. Haupt Garden 58
   National Museum of African Art 57
   National Museum of the American Indian 54
   National Zoo 32, 112
   Renwick Gallery 99
   shopping 89
   Smithsonian American Art Museum 96
   Smithsonian Folklife Festival 72
Smoking 122
Soccer 61
Southwest Waterfront 71
Sports 60–61
Stabler-Leadbeater Apothecary Museum 113
Stanton, Elizabeth Cady 15
Star-Spangled Banner 23

Statue of Freedom 12, 15
Statues 51
Stuart, Gilbert 25
Studio Theatre 67
Supreme Court Building 49, 80

T

Tanner, Henry Ossawa 18
Taxes 125
Taxis 120, 121
Tayloe, John III 100
Tennis 61
Theaters 66–7
   Arena Stage 66
   Children's Theater 70
   Folger Shakespeare Theatre 66, 79, 81
   Ford's Theatre 48, 66, 95
   Gala Hispanic Theatre 67
   Harman Center for the Arts 67
   Kennedy Center 5, 6, 66, 99
   National Theatre 67
   Shakespeare Free for All 72
   Shakespeare Theatre 66
   Studio Theatre 67
   Warner Theatre 67
   Wolftrap Children's Theatre in the Woods 64
   Woolly Mammoth Theatre Company 67
Theodore Roosevelt Island 59
Thornton, Dr. William 14, 100
Tickets, budget 71
Tidal Basin 90
Time zone 124
Tomb of the Unknown Soldier 34
Tourist information 125
Trains 118, 119

Travel 71, 118–21
Travelers with Specific Requirements 123
Travel insurance 122
Treasury Building 49, 100
Trips from Washington, DC 74–5
Truman, Harry S. 19
Trumball, John 15
Tubman, Harriet 47
Tudor Place 107
Twain, Mark 99
Tysons Corner Center and Tysons Galleria 69, 114

U
U Street, NW 5, 112
Ulysses S. Grant Memorial 51, 82
Union Station 70, 79
US Botanic Garden 6, 58, 71, 80
US Capitol 6, 8–9, 10, **12–15**, 79
  Capitol Grounds 82
  history 14
  Statue of Freedom 12, 15
  walking tour 70
US Constitution 14, 42, 43, 55, 62
United States Holocaust Memorial Museum 54–5, 86–7, 90
Universities
  George Washington University 100
  Georgetown University 106
University of Maryland Athletics 61

V
Vaccinations 122
Vermeer, Johannes 24, 26
Vermilion 68, 115
Vietnam Veterans Memorial 7, 50–51, 86
Visas 122, 123
Visitor information 125

W
Walking 121
Walking tours 70, 71
Walter, Thomas U. 14
War of 1812 14, 42
Warner Theatre 67
Washington, George 44, 65
  Arlington House 34
  Bishop's Garden 31
  Chesapeake and Ohio Canal 105
  Christ Church 113
  Gadsby's Tavern Museum 48
  George Washington University 100
  George Washington's Distillery 63
  Mount Vernon 7, 36–9, 111
  portraits of 14, 25, 44
  tomb 39
  United States Capitol 14, 101
  White House 16, 19
Washington, Martha 36, 37, 39, 45
Washington, Walter E. 47
Washington Capitals 61
Washington Football Team 61
Washington Harbour 105, 107
Washington Monument 5, 6, 7, 50, 87
Washington Mystics 61
Washington National Cathedral 11, **30–31**, 111
  Christmas services 72
  exploring Washington, DC 7
  schools 112
Washington Nationals 73
Washington Wizards 61
Watergate Hotel 102
Watson and the Shark (Copley) 24

Weather 124
Wells-Barnett, Ida B. 47
Westend Bistro 68, 103
Wharf, The 112
Whistler, James McNeill 57, 89
White House 6, 10, **16–19**, 99, 101
  decorative features 18
  Easter Egg Roll 73
  exploring Washington, DC 7
  President Truman's renovations 19
White House and Foggy Bottom 98–103
  map 98–9
  restaurants 103
Wi-Fi 124
Williamsburg 75
Wilson, Woodrow 48
Wilson, Mrs Woodrow 18
Winfield, Rodney 30
Wisconsin Avenue 105
Wolf Trap National Park for the Performing Arts 67
Wolftrap Children's Theatre in the Woods 64
Woodrow Wilson House 48
Woolly Mammoth Theatre Company 67
World War I 51
World War II 43
  United States Holocaust Memorial Museum 54–5, 86–7, 90
  World War II Memorial 51, 88
Wright, Frank Lloyd 49
Wright brothers 20, 21

Z
Zoos
  National Zoo 7, 11, 64, 70, 112
  O. Orkin Insect Zoo 90

Acknowledgments

Author

Ron Burke is the author or co-author of 19 books. A former Capitol Hill resident, he was born in the Washington, DC metropolitan area and has lived here most of his life.

Susan Burke lives in Virginia, where she worked on a daily newspaper for 20 years before becoming an editor for the Air Line Pilots Association. She is also a freelance editor for journals on labor, economics, and art conservation.

Additional contributor
Paul Franklin, Nancy Mikula

Publishing Director Georgina Dee

Publisher Vivien Antwi

Design Director Phil Ormerod

Editorial Michelle Crane, Rebecca Flynn, Rachel Fox, Fay Franklin, Fíodhna Ní Ghríofa, Freddie Marriage, Scarlett O'Hara, Marianne Petrou, Sally Schafer, Christine Stroyan

Cover Design Maxine Pedliham, Vinita Venugopal

Design Marisa Renzullo, Jaynan Spengler

Picture Research Phoebe Lowndes, Susie Peachey, Ellen Root, Oran Tarjan

Cartography Subhashree Bharti, Simonetta Giori, Suresh Kumar, Casper Morris, John Plumer

DTP Jason Little, George Nimmo, Azeem Siddiqui, Joanna Stenlake

Production Nancy-Jane Maun

Factchecker Alice Powers

Proofreader Alyson Silverwood

Indexer Hilary Bird

Illustrator Chris Orr & Associates

First edition created by Sargasso Media Ltd, London

Revisions Parnika Bagla, Subhashree Bharti, Marta Bescos, Emma Brady, Neha Chander, Dipika Dasgupta, Mohammad Hassan, Bharti Karakoti, Stephen Keeling, Nayan Keshan, Taiyaba Khatoon, Sumita Khatwani, Shikha Kulkarni, Rachel Laidler, Bhavika Mathur, Nancy Mikula, Chhavi Nagpal, Todd Obolsky, Bandana Paul, Alice Powers, Vagisha Pushp, Anuroop Sanwalia, Ankita Sharma, Mark Silas, Aakanksha Singh, Rituraj Singh, Akanksha Siwach, Beverly Smart, Manjari Thakur, Priyanka Thakur, Rachel Thompson, Stuti Tiwari, Ankita Awasthi Tröger, Vaishali Vashisht, Åsa Westerlund, Tanveer Zaidi

Commissioned Photography: Paul Franklin, Rough Guides/Angus Osborn, Rough Guides/Paul Whitfield, Kim Sayer, Giles Stokoe

Picture Credits

The publisher would like to thank the following for their kind permission to reproduce their photographs:

(Key: a-above; b-below/bottom; c-center; f-far; l-left; r-right; t-top)

Alamy Images: Rubens Alarcon 102bc; Alpha Stock 82br; B Christopher 102cla; David Coleman 57cb, 59tl; dbimages 101cl; Danita Delimont 49cl;

EggImages 73tr; Marshall Ikonography 107br; Nikreates 3tr, 106–7t, 116–117; North Wind Picture Archives 14tr, 42t; PAINTING/ 18cr, / Edgar Degas Dancers at the Barre. Circa 1900. Oil on canvas. Phillips Collection, Washington, D.C. 56tl; Wiliam Perry 59bc; Pictures Now 13tr; Edwin Remsberg 114tl; Stock Connection Blue 60b; Terry Smith Images 58t; Michael Ventura 4cla; Visions of America/Purestock 111br; Michael Wald 33bc; Harry Walker 61tr; YAY Media AS 43tr.

Alamy Stock Photo: age fotostock/Tono Balahuer 105tr; Kristina Blokhin 90br; Rob Crandall 106clb; Paul Christian Gordon 72tl; Ken Howard 67cl.

Brasserie Beck/RW Restaurant Group: Scott Suchman 97tr.

Clyde's Restaurant Group: 109br.

Corbis: Bettmann 42br; Gary Carter 29tl; Design Pics/Robert Bartow 2tr, 40–41; Hulton-Deutsch Collection 43clb; LOOP IMAGES/John Greim 4crb, 63br, 111t; Oscar White 19tl; Richard T. Nowitz 62cb; PictureNet 4cr; Rudy Sulgan 51bl; Terra/Fred Ward 28clb.

Dorling Kindersley: The Three Servicemen Statue © Frederick Hart /Vietnam Veterans Memorial Fund, 1984 86bl; John F. Kennedy Monument, 1971 ©Robert Berks Studios, Inc. All Rights reserved 98tl.

Dreamstime.com: Americanspirit 36cla; Tonya Aragon 7tr; Avmedved 16–17t, 59cr, 87bl; Jon Bilous 31tr, 71clb; Olga Bogatyrenko 12–13c; Brandon Bourdages © Vietnam Veterans Memorial Fund 50bl; Orhan Çam 79tr; Ken Cole 49tr; Cvandyke 64b; Dinhhang 11cla, 105br; Mesut Doğan 4clb; Erix2005 88tl; F11photo 4t, 28br, 34–5c, 52–3; Alexandre Fagundes De Fagundes 39bl, 51tr, 110tl; Julie Feinstein 58bl; Anton Foltin 74t; Frankljunior 70bl; Jose Gil 45tr; Diego Grandi 11cra; Richard Gunion 72 br; Christian Hinkle 113clb; Izanbar 2tl, 8–9, 74bl; Jemaerca 7crb; Ritu Jethani 10crb, 81tl, 96c; Wangkun Jia 11tl, 96br; Kenk 75c; Stephanie Kenner 100cla; Steve Kingsman 86t; Klodien 75tr; Kmiragaya 35cr; Anna Krivitskaia 64tl; Richie Lomba 46tr; Lunamarina 3tl, 76–77; Maisna66br; Mkopka 112b; Mvogel 55tl; Nam Nguyen 71tr; Nickjene 100bl; Nyker1 61cl; Oleksii Popov/Panvik D. Roosevelt and his Dog Fala 1997 © Neil Estern 50t; Zhi Qi 54bl, 56b; Sborisov 4b; Steveheap 4cl; Vacclav 6cla; Jixue Yang 4ca; Jakub Zajic 70t.

Equinox Restaurant: 103bl.

Ford's Theatre Society: 93c, 94tl; Maxwell MacKenzie 48tr, 66t.

Fotolia: FD 15bc.

George Washington's Mount Vernon: 11bl, 36br, 36–7c.

Getty Images: Hulton Archive 47tr; Buyenlarge/ Carol M. Highsmith 47clb; Corbis NX / Richard T. Nowitz 92–3; Sean Gallup 45bl; Hisham Ibrahim/ George Mason National Memorial 2002 Artist: Wendy M. Ross, Ross Sculpture Studio LLC, 6611 Landon Lane, Bethesda, Md. 20817 rosssculpturestudio.com 62tl; Popperfoto 44cb; Tim Sloan 12bl; Chip Somodevilla 67tr; Julie